HURWITZ

W0082058

ACTOR'S CHOICE:
SCENES FOR TEENS

EDITED BY
JASON PIZZARELLO

Copyright © 2010 Playscripts, Inc. All rights reserved.

Any unauthorized copying of this book or excerpts from this book is strictly forbidden by law. No part of this book may be reproduced, stored in a retrieval system or transmitted in any form, by any means now known or yet to be invented, including photocopying or scanning, without prior permission from the publisher.

Actor's Choice: Scenes for Teens is published by Playscripts, Inc., 450 Seventh Avenue, Suite 809, New York, New York, 10123, www.playscripts.com

Cover design by Michael Minichiello
Text design and layout by Kimberly Lew

First Edition: September 2010
10 9 8 7 6 5 4 3 2 1

CAUTION: These scenes are intended for audition and classroom use; permission is not required for those purposes only. The plays represented in this book (the "Plays") are fully protected under the copyright laws of the United States of America and of all countries with which the United States has reciprocal copyright relations, whether through bilateral or multilateral treaties or otherwise, and including, but not limited to, all countries covered by the Berne Convention, the Pan-American Copyright Convention and the Universal Copyright Convention. All rights, including, without limitation, professional and amateur stage rights; motion picture, recitation, lecturing, public reading, radio broadcasting, television, video or sound recording rights; rights to all other forms of mechanical or electronic reproduction not known or yet to be invented, such as CD-ROM, CD-I, DVD, information storage and retrieval systems and photocopying; and the rights of translation into non-English languages, are strictly reserved. Amateur and stock performance rights to the Plays are controlled exclusively by Playscripts, Inc. ("Playscripts"). All licensing requests and inquiries concerning amateur and stock performance rights should be addressed to Playscripts (see contact information above). Inquiries concerning all other rights should be addressed to Playscripts, as well; such inquiries will be communicated to the author and the author's agent, as applicable. The Plays may include references to brand names and trademarks owned by third parties, and may include references to public figures. Playscripts is not necessarily affiliated with these public figures, or with the owners of such trademarks and brand names. Such references are included solely for parody, political comment or other permitted purposes.

Editor's Note: In some of the scenes in this book, dialogue or stage directions from the play may have been removed for clarity's sake.

Library of Congress Cataloging-in-Publication Data

Actor's choice : scenes for teens / edited by Jason Pizzarello.
    p. cm.
Summary: "Collection of scenes from the Playscripts, Inc. catalog of plays, representing a variety of American playwrights. The source material for each scene may be found on the Playscripts website, where nearly the entire text of every play can be read for free. Intended for teenage actors"--Provided by publisher.
ISBN 978-0-9819099-4-3
1. Monologues. 2. Acting--Auditions. 3. Teenagers--Drama. I. Pizzarello, Jason, 1980-
PN2080.A2875 2010
808.82'45--dc22

                                        2010019464

Table of Contents

Scenes for One Man and One Woman

A Scene for Either

Editor's Note

With 1500+ plays published in our catalog, we at Playscripts felt it was about time to create our very first scene collection. There was a wealth of engaging material to choose from, and we're proud to present these exciting selections to you now.

Scenes for Teens pulls together short scenes (under 10 minutes) for a specific group of actors (age 13-19). From hilarious spoofs to classic adaptations, you will discover a variety of genres throughout the book. It is our hope that you find these scenes perfect for use in class, competitions, and auditions.

For easy reference, an indication of the comedic or dramatic sensibility of each scene can be found in the Table of Contents. The material in this book is further broken into four categories: *Scenes for Two Women*, *Scenes for Two Men*, *Scenes for One Man and One Woman*, and *A Scene for Either* (gender).

Although these scenes will give you a glimpse into the world of the play, to fully understand the context of your scene, you need the play itself at your fingertips. That's what sets the *Actor's Choice* series above the rest. For every scene, you have the option of reading up to 90% of the entire play, all from one source, and all for free. Simply visit the Playscripts website at *www.playscripts.com*.

On behalf of Playscripts and all the exceptional playwrights represented in this book, I hope that you enjoy these scenes!

—Jason Pizzarello, Publications Director
Playscripts, Inc.

SPECIAL THANKS

This book was made possible by all of the talented playwrights who allowed us to include scenes from their wonderful plays.

Special thanks are due to Kimberly Lew, Sarah Bernstein, Erin Salvi, BC, Michael Minichiello, and Jon Jory for their contributions to the creation of this book. Thanks also to William Repicci, for the opportunity.

Tips for Student Actors by Jon Jory

Ten ways to tune your performance

1. *Concentration.* While you're acting, keep your mind on the stage and in the circumstances. You have to be completely aware of what the other actors are doing and how your character would react to them. To focus wavering concentration, give yourself small achievable tasks onstage, inside the story. The woman over there is your "mother"? What exactly is she wearing? What does your character want her to do right now? Drag your mind onto the stage and keep it there.

2. *Be aware of rhythm.* The actor's work is much like that of the jazz musician. Every play, every scene, every speech needs mixed rhythms. Look for the quick part in the slow, nostalgic memory speech. Look for the pause in the hard-driving, angry argument. Reinvest new acting energy at the point where the subject changes or the conversation veers off. You need to find the sensible variety in speed and tone. Say to yourself, "Let's do a little jazz here!"

3. *Get the part in your body.* What your mind thinks, what your emotions feel, all of this is supposed to show up in your body. Acting is doing. Don't know how? Start with a simple physical task accompanying your speech. Stretch, do some easy exercises while you talk to your sister about last night's game. At the very least it will signal to your body that it's expected to show up. In most cases, no body means no acting.

4. *Ever heard the term "self-reacting"?* You do it all the time in life but you probably don't do it enough on stage. Here's how it works: while you talk you have opinions about what you're saying and how you're saying it. You start a sentence describing an automobile accident. Suddenly you realize you left a detail out, and you stop in mid-sentence and readjust. Or you're talking and you say something even you think is stupid, and you make a face that lets the other person in on your new opinion of what you just said. These are just a few examples.

5. *Tone.* It goes this way: you're doing the balcony scene in *Romeo and Juliet* and you're locked in the "love" tone. You give every line you say a particular sound that reeks of roses and heartshaped chocolates. The whole scene is being played in the love tone. There are other favorite tones, including the "angry" tone, the "memory" tone, the "tragic" tone, the "dominant" tone, etc. Get out of the tone and into the scene.

6. *Words mean something.* Sometimes I go to the theatre and get lulled into a somnolent state by a river of words that seem to have no personal meaning to the actor. The words seem colorless, containers filled with a transparent fluid. The good actor makes the words signify. When she says "Aunt Helen," you can picture Aunt Helen, remote, cynical, and overbearing. Part of this is simple

emphasis. The sentence you're saying means entirely different things depending on the word or words you choose to stress. You need to invest meaning in the words you say, you need to energize them and sometimes roll the sound of them around in your mouth. Don't just let the words lie there. They need you.

7. *Variety.* Here's a real and continual secret of the trade: don't be anything all the time. Don't be angry all the time, don't be sweet all the time, don't be passive all the time, don't be aggressive all the time. Don't treat the other characters all the same way. Life is changeable, and so is the personality of your character. Don't sit down all the time, don't stand up all the time, don't be still all the time or active all the time. When the audience thinks they know what you're going to do next they are less interested.

8. *The pause.* Silence is the actor's condiment. It adds flavor where you need it. Remember that language is born out of silence. Silence is the gestation period for words. After a long line of words and sentences, a pause often refreshes the listeners and refocuses them. The important pause occurs when what you want is so balanced by the difficulty of getting it that you have a profound need to think it over before you can go on. Think about the possibilities for these pauses as you rehearse. They can define the role.

9. *I know she knows I know.* When you're playing a scene in which the characters know each other well and probably have for a long time, you have to be careful to play in a way that acknowledges that almost anything you say has a history. For instance, when you talk about a mutual friend to your brother, you already know what his attitude toward that person is and you take that into account as you talk. It is this understanding of each other that defines scenes where the two characters have a history together.

10. *Don't drop the end of the line.* Be careful that the strong verbal energy you start with doesn't gradually dissipate, so that near the end of the sentence or speech you have run out of gas. One of the reasons that this small flaw can deeply affect your playing is that playwrights often put the most important and colorful information at the end of the line. Drop the end of the line and you obscure or lose the sense of the line.

Finally, remember that as a good craftsperson you don't use every tool on every job. Practice will refine your sense of what tool will solve a current problem.

This material is drawn from an article that was originally published in Dramatics *magazine.*

Jon Jory, the celebrated artistic director of Actors Theatre of Louisville for thirty-one years, is now teaching acting and directing at the University of Washington. Several of his plays are published by Playscripts, Inc.

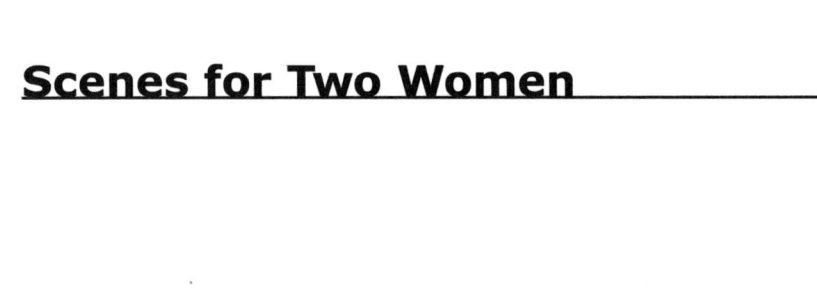

Scenes for Two Women

FASHIONISTAS
A NARCISSISTIC LOVE STORY

by Janet Allard

Characters

ECHO, a teenage girl. A misfit. Desperately wants to speak but can't initiate a conversation or express desire unless someone else expresses it first.

CALLIOPE, an outsider for the way she dresses. Sort of a hippie who shops at thrift stores.

Scene

As the fashion elite prepare for the runway show of the season, Calliope plots to destroy it—P.E.T.A.-style. She attempts to enlist Echo's help, but finds her thoughts turned more toward the handsome Narcissus than animal rights.

> *(CALLIOPE and ECHO in the ladies room.*
>
> *ECHO picks at her electric guitar.*
>
> *CALLIOPE pours red paint [that looks like blood] into water balloons.)*

CALLIOPE. Okay this time, it's gonna work. We're gonna take out the whole line of models in the finale. You're gonna help me right?

ECHO. *(Not listening.)* Right.

CALLIOPE. Water-balloons full of blood. I'm a genius.

ECHO. Genius.

CALLIOPE. You know, the thing is—Donatella wouldn't club a baby seal, she wouldn't have the stomach for it. I bet she doesn't even cook her own meat for dinner, I bet she thinks veal is a vegetable.

But, she can wear animal's skin to get a compliment. Hypocrite.
She doesn't see the blood she's shedding.
All the blood. Who gave us the right to kill for fashion? People are so disgusting. What if someone took your baby and skinned it and made it into a coat, how would you feel, we don't even think like that, we're so absorbed with ourselves and how we look, so in love with ourselves we'll kill a furry little cute animal just to get a compliment. It's social survival, survival of the fittest, and if you want to take down a fashionista you've got to hit 'em where it hurts. Public humiliation. That's the name of the game.

There is only one way to stop them.
To stop the vanity! Put an end to Narcissus!—the clothing line I mean.
Are you even listening?

ECHO. Listening.

CALLIOPE. You're not, you're probably thinking why is she such a raving lunatic, let the animals die, I don't care.

ECHO. I don't care.

CALLIOPE. But you do. Deep down. If you paid attention, hello, Echo, are you going to help me with this or not?

ECHO. Not.

CALLIOPE. Chicken. Where are you going?

ECHO. Going.

CALLIOPE. To chase Narcissus around, right?

ECHO. Right.

CALLIOPE. To stand around waiting for him to notice you, right?

ECHO. Right.

CALLIOPE. If you're like, so hung up on him, you should tell him.

ECHO. Tell him?

CALLIOPE. What? Is that so crazy, if he's in love with you too, don't you want to know?

ECHO. No.

> *(Pause.)*

CALLIOPE. Do you ever start anything, Echo? You know, Initiate?

ECHO. Initiate?

CALLIOPE. Yeah, you know, DO something? Take action? You know?

ECHO. No.

CALLIOPE. Yeah, that's what I thought, that's your problem, all you do is respond. You react. You let everyone else DO. And you copy them. Nobody respects you and you never get what you want. Sorry if that's harsh but I'm right aren't I. I'm trying to help you out here, as a friend.

ECHO. A friend.

CALLIOPE. Yeah, I'm telling you the truth. You hide out, you lurk around in abandoned places, in empty hallways and bathrooms, you never say what's on your mind, really. You hide. Is that any way to live? You'll never get noticed, that way you know, you've got to take action.

ECHO. Action.

CALLIOPE. Yeah, you don't have a chance in hell with Narcissus. I'm telling you the truth. But don't you want to find that out? Instead of going around all silent and hung up on him, hoping for something that's never going to happen.

ECHO. Never going to happen?

CALLIOPE. Or maybe he's in love with you and you're sitting in this bathroom wasting your life. You should confront him.

ECHO. Confront him?

CALLIOPE. Open up to him. Meet him in some dark hallway. Grab him.

ECHO. Grab him?

CALLIOPE. Grab him and Kiss him.

ECHO. Kiss him.

CALLIOPE. Yeah, surprise him, why not? Tell him.

ECHO. Why not tell him.

CALLIOPE. Exactly. What's the worst that could happen? If he rejects you so what?

ECHO. So what.

CALLIOPE. Then you can move on. That's life that's how we live.

ECHO. We live.

CALLIOPE. That's right, Echo, we live, we love that's what we do. And if he doesn't love you, maybe there's someone else who will. Someone better. Echo?

> *(But she's gone.)*

ANTIGONE NOW

by Melissa Cooper
inspired by Sophocles' *Antigone*

Characters

ANTIGONE, still a teenager.

ISMENE, her sister, a few years older.

Scene

The city is in chaos following a civil war waged by Polyneices and Eteocles, brothers of Antigone and Ismene. After the brothers kill each other in battle, Creon, the girls' uncle, seizes control of the city and orders that the body of Polyneices remain unburied to show what happens to traitors and rebels. Antigone is determined to bury her brother, even in the face of death, and comes to her sister for help.

> *(ISMENE is alone inside her apartment, late at night. She puts on head-phones or turns on a boom box. Music blasts on, a loud, relentless contemporary sound. Maybe hip-hop or rap. ISMENE dances fiercely, determined to lose herself in the music. ANTIGONE is outside in the street, dodging snipers and explosions as she makes her way to stand outside ISMENE's apartment building.)*

ANTIGONE. *(Hollering at Ismene's door as many times as necessary:)* Ismene! Ismene!

> *(ISMENE finally hears her sister's voice. She snaps off the music, and races to the door to pull ANTIGONE inside to safety.)*

ISMENE. Antigone. Get in. What are you doing outside after curfew?

ANTIGONE. Why does suffering never end? It just goes on and on and on…

ISMENE. Calm down. Did something happen?

ANTIGONE. Yes, something happened. Of course, something happened.

ISMENE. Don't snap at me. I didn't do anything.

ANTIGONE. No. You sit inside with your doors and windows sealed, blaring music to drown out the sirens. You have no idea what's going on out there.

ISMENE. I do so.

ANTIGONE. All right, tell me. *(She waits a beat, then goes on.)*

15

See? You can't say anything, because you don't know. I'm opening your windows, Ismene.

ISMENE. No, no…

ANTIGONE. Let the sounds and smells roll in—

ISMENE. *(Grappling with her sister to keep her from opening the windows:)* Get away from the windows.

ANTIGONE. —so you'll know what I know.

ISMENE. I'll tell you what I know. I know the war is over and our brothers are dead.

ANTIGONE. Old news already.

ISMENE. I know Creon is king—

ANTIGONE. Yesterday's paper.

ISMENE. I know people are hungry—

ANTIGONE. You call that news?

ISMENE. —and Creon's troops are prowling the city—

ANTIGONE. Go on…

ISMENE. *(Pointedly:)* They're rounding up traitors and troublemakers.

ANTIGONE. And—? Is that all you know?

ISMENE. I know you're addicted to suffering. You go looking for trouble, then wail and moan when you find it. Well, I've had enough. The war is over, and I'm going to be happy.

> *(ISMENE turns on the music again. Loud. She moves to the beat until ANTIGONE switches it off.)*

ANTIGONE. Saying you've had enough doesn't change what's happening out there. I saw.
I saw with my own eyes. I can't un-see what I saw. I can't un-know—

ISMENE. *(Realizing something really has happened to ANTIGONE:)* What is it you saw, sweetheart?

ANTIGONE. Our brothers.

ISMENE. Our brothers? Where?

ANTIGONE. I saw our brothers, dead in the street. Their arms and legs were all tangled together, like when they were little and they used to wrestle. Except the blood is real, and they don't get up.
I hid behind a gate. Creon's men came and pried apart the bodies. They poured water over Eteocles' wounds, and washed away the dust and blood. They laid him in a cart, and took him away to be buried with honor.

ISMENE. And Polyneices?

ANTIGONE. Lies where he fell, like trash in the street.

ISMENE. They'll come back for him, sweetheart. You wait and see.

ANTIGONE. No, they won't. No, they won't. No one may bury him, no one may touch him. It's against the law.

ISMENE. What are you talking about?

ANTIGONE. Creon has forbidden it.
Poor body, poor brother. Holes in his chest, Ismene, and the birds are so hungry. After the soldiers left, I threw stones at the buzzards, but they wouldn't leave. On my way home, I passed starving dogs, rooting for food. They'll find him soon—

ISMENE. Quiet, love, sshh… You're not thinking right. You misunderstood. They're coming back for Polyneices. When dawn comes, we'll go out together and then you'll see, it was all a mistake.

ANTIGONE. When dawn comes, Creon will be here to tell the whole city—to tell you, Ismene, and me—that anyone who touches the dead man will die.
So, Ismene, that's the way it is. Now, what are you going to do about it?

ISMENE. If everything you say is true, there's nothing I can do.

ANTIGONE. You can help me in my work.

ISMENE. What work?

ANTIGONE. Help me bury our brother.

ISMENE. We can't bury him. You just told me it's against the law.

ANTIGONE. Creon's law. It's nothing.

ISMENE. *(Fiercely:)* It's not nothing. The law's not nothing. You can die for it. That's not nothing.

ANTIGONE. Ismene, our brother is rotting in the street.

ISMENE. Slow down, little one. Stop and think—

ANTIGONE. What's wrong with you? I hear the birds screaming, and the dogs—

ISMENE. You need to rest.

ANTIGONE. No—

ISMENE. Rest for a minute, sweetheart. Just one minute.

ANTIGONE. *(Despite herself, beginning to yield:)* I'm so tired.

ISMENE. I know. You're so tired.

ANTIGONE. For a minute I'll rest. But just for a minute.

ISMENE. Just for a minute. We'll both rest.

> *(ISMENE holds ANTIGONE in her arms.)*

It's been so long since I slept. I mean, really slept.

ANTIGONE. How long?

ISMENE. Long time. Before the war.

ANTIGONE. Before the war. When Mama was alive, and Daddy could see…

ISMENE. Yes.

ANTIGONE. I slept then, too. I slept and slept.

ISMENE. Curl up close, like on Mama's lap. Such soft hair. Such a little package.

ANTIGONE. Mmm. Nice. Tell me a story.

ISMENE. What kind of story?

ANTIGONE. You know. How things used to be. Before.

ISMENE. Before. Once upon a time…

ANTIGONE. Tell me something I never knew.

ISMENE. *(After a moment:)* Mama used to paint my toenails, the palest shade of pink. Then she'd put her face down close to my feet and her hair would tickle my ankles and she'd blow little warm storms of breath on my toes to dry them. We'd put our feet together, side by side, and mine were so small.

ANTIGONE. Where am I in the story?

ISMENE. After you were born, she'd hold you up so your tiny feet dangled next to mine, and then I knew how big I really was. I blew my breath on your toes then, and you pulled at my hair, and laughed.
You never knew that before.

ANTIGONE. No, I never knew that before.

ISMENE. Now sleep.

> *(The sisters sleep. ANTIGONE's eyes fly open. She sees the ghost of Polyneices. He is moving away from her.)*

ANTIGONE. *(Awake and on her feet:)* Polyneices!

ISMENE. *(Trying desperately to stay asleep:)* Go back to sleep, baby. Please.

ANTIGONE. My head's exploding. I'm on fire.

> *(ANTIGONE shakes and prods ISMENE to wake her.)*

Ismene, do you believe in ghosts?

ISMENE. *(Still refusing to yield her moment of rest:)* Ghosts are just bad dreams.

ANTIGONE. I can't sleep anymore, but I'm dreaming all the time. The second my eyes close, boom! the dreams start. Sometimes the dreams start *while* my eyes are closing, and then, for a flash of a second, I'm living in two worlds at once.

ISMENE. You live in the same world as everyone else.

ANTIGONE. I'm going to bury Polyneices.

ISMENE. *(Fully awake and engaged now:)* No.

ANTIGONE. Watch me.

ISMENE. You can't. Look at yourself. You're not strong enough.

ANTIGONE. So I'll do as much as I can, and when I can't do anymore, I'll stop.

ISMENE. Why start something when you know you can't finish? It's just looking for trouble.

ANTIGONE. Trouble doesn't scare me.

ISMENE. You're not the only sister who's lost a brother, you know.

ANTIGONE. But this one is *my* brother.

ISMENE. And mine. All your dead are my dead too.

ANTIGONE. Then how can you just leave him there?

ISMENE. Because he's dead and we're alive.

(She takes ANTIGONE's hand and blows her breath onto it.)

Feel that? Breath. Life. We survived. You and me, Antigone and Ismene. We're alive. We can start again—

ANTIGONE. Oh, yes, we'll start again, we'll work, we'll find lovers, we'll be happy—

ISMENE. It could happen…

ANTIGONE. You know, Ismene, if you come crawling to me now on your hands and knees, *begging* to help, I'll say, "No."

ISMENE. Antigone—

ANTIGONE. No. You don't get it. You can't. For you there's nothing but what you can taste and touch and smell. But there are other worlds than this one, and those worlds have their own laws. I'm going to bury my brother.

CHICKEN BONES FOR THE TEENAGE SOUP

by Alan Haehnel

Characters

KIMMY

KELLY

Scene

Kimmy and Kelly, dressed almost identically, are sitting together in a corner of the school cafeteria. The scene starts bubbly and ends homicidally.

KIMMY. Kelly, you are my very best friend. You are amazing.

KELLY. Kimmy, you know I feel the same way about you.

KIMMY. I will always love you. I mean it. You know, Bridget gave me one of her school pictures yesterday, one of the little wallet-sized ones, and she wrote on the back of it "best friends forever." But she doesn't really mean it. She was just writing that.

KELLY. She wrote that on mine, too.

KIMMY. No way.

KELLY. Yes way.

KIMMY. See, that's what I mean. Some friends go around writing that stuff and saying that stuff to everybody, but they don't mean it. But when I say it to you, and when I write it on the back of the 8x10 school photo I give you, you know I really mean it. "Kimmy and Kelly, best friends always."

KELLY. Forever.

KIMMY. And ever.

KELLY / KIMMY. Amen.

KIMMY. See? That shows what amazing friends we are, when we finish…

KELLY. Each other's sentences?

KIMMY. Yes! We're like one person…

KELLY. Inside two bodies?

KIMMY. Yes! I mean, sometimes when I'm talking to you I just feel as if I'm talking to myself.

KELLY. I know what you mean. And how many times have we worn practically exactly the same thing to school and we didn't even call each other?

KIMMY. I know it! We have the same tastes in foods, the same tastes in music…

KELLY. The same tastes in fashion, the same tastes in guys.

KIMMY. Yeah, we do, don't we?

KELLY. We're the luckiest two people on earth, to have each other as friends. That first day in kindergarten, the first day I met you, it was like a cloud just opened up and the sun came shining through and I knew we were going to be like twins.

KIMMY. Yeah. I remember that. We both had *Powerpuff Girl* coloring books. And what color was it that we both had missing from our crayon sets?

KELLY. Yellow.

KIMMY. Yellow. That was amazing. We both came in with exactly the same crayon missing.

KELLY. Fate.

KIMMY. Destiny.

KELLY. True, true friendship. We're going to the same college, aren't we?

KIMMY. You better believe it! We'll both major in psychology…

KELLY. And we'll graduate together and become famous psychologists…

KIMMY. And we'll have offices next door to each other! We'll call ourselves Kimmy and Kelly, Best Friends Psychology.

KELLY. I like that. That's perfect.

KIMMY. You're perfect, Kelly.

KELLY. So are you, Kimmy.

KIMMY. But you know what, Kelly?

KELLY. What, Kimmy?

KIMMY. If I ever catch you flirting with Marco again, all of that won't mean crap.

KELLY. What?

KIMMY. You know what I'm talking about!

KELLY. Hey, if anybody was flirting with anybody, he was flirting with me. Can I help it if he just happens to find me attractive?

KIMMY. Why he would find a fat cow attractive, I have no idea!

KELLY. Maybe it's because he's stuck with a bloated, self-centered witch!

KIMMY. Me, self-centered? Look who's talking, Miss Drama Queen!

KELLY. Oh, look in the mirror, why don't you? You make me sick!

KIMMY. Stay away from Marco!

KELLY. Make me!

KIMMY. I hate you!

KELLY. Not as much as I hate you!

    (They grab one another by the hair.)

EMMA

adapted by Jon Jory
from the novel by Jane Austen

Characters

HARRIET, sweet and modest.

EMMA, wealthy, charming and vivacious.

Scene

Emma, a self-proclaimed matchmaker, is set on finding a suitable husband for her new friend Harriet. Though her brother-in-law and confidante Mr. Knightley discourages her, Emma has convinced Harriet to reject an offer of marriage from the respectable Mr. Martin and to instead seek the affections of Frank Churchill, who in turn has shown a marked interest in Emma. Emma and Harriet both have just separately discovered that Frank Churchill has been secretly engaged for some time.

HARRIET. Dear Miss Woodhouse, is not this the oddest news that ever was?

EMMA. What news do you mean?

HARRIET. About Jane Fairfax. Did you ever hear anything so strange? I met Mr. Weston just now and he told me.

EMMA. Harriet… He told you what?

HARRIET. That Jane Fairfax and Mr. Frank Churchill have been privately engaged this long while and are to be married.

EMMA. *(Amazed at HARRIET's cheerful and animated behavior:)* Yes, I see.

HARRIET. Had you any idea of his being in love with her? You, perhaps, might. You who can see into everybody's heart.

EMMA. Upon my word, I begin to doubt my having any such talent. Can you seriously ask me, Harriet, if I thought him attached at the very time I was—tacitly if not openly—encouraging you to give way to your feelings? You may be very sure if I had I should have cautioned you accordingly.

HARRIET. Me! Surely you do not think I care about Mr. Frank Churchill?

EMMA. You do not mean to deny that you gave me reason to understand that you did care about him.

HARRIET. Him!— Never, never. Dear Miss Woodhouse, how could you so mistake me?

EMMA. Harriet! Mistake you— Am I to suppose then...

HARRIET. I know we agreed never to name him—but considering how infinitely superior he is to everybody else. Mr. Frank Churchill, indeed! I hope I have better taste than to think of Mr. Frank Churchill, who is like nobody by his side.

EMMA. Harriet...

HARRIET. At first, if you had not told me that more wonderful things had happened; that there had been matches of greater disparity, I should not have dared.

EMMA. Wait, let us understand each other now, without the possibility of further mistake. Are you speaking of Mr. Knightly?

HARRIET. To be sure I am. I never had an idea of anybody else. When we talked about him, it was clear as possible.

EMMA. All you said appeared to me to relate to a different person. I could almost assert that you had named Mr. Churchill. I am sure the service he had rendered you, in protecting you from the Gypsies, was spoken of.

HARRIET. Oh, Miss Woodhouse, how you do forget!

EMMA. My dear Harriet, I perfectly remember. I told you that I did not wonder at your attachment; that considering the service he had rendered you, it was extremely natural, and you agreed.

HARRIET. Oh dear! Now I recollect what you mean; but I was thinking of something very different at the time. Indeed not the gypsies but of Mr. Knightly's coming and asking me to dance, when Mr. Elton would not stand up with me. That was the service which made me begin to feel how superior he was to every other being on earth.

(EMMA turns away.)

I hope Miss Woodhouse that if... After all they were your own words... 'Matches of greater disparity had taken place.' And if Mr. Knightly should really—if he does not mind the disparity I hope you will not set yourself against it. You are too good for that, I am sure.

EMMA. Have you any idea of Mr. Knightly returning your affection?

HARRIET. I must say that I have. I have been conscious of a difference in behavior ever since that dance. He talks to me a good deal more than he used to and his manner is much changed... Kinder and sweeter. Only two days ago he praised me for being without art or affectation...

(EMMA moves off to the square but HARRIET goes on speaking as if she was still there.)

He often removes from his chair to one closer to mine... Most clearly, he walked apart with me at the strawberry picking... And spoke to me in a more particular way than he had ever done. He seemed to be almost asking me whether my affections were engaged.

EMMA. *(Returning:)* Might he not... Is it not possible that when enquiring as you thought, into the state of your affections, he might be alluding to Mr. Martin.

HARRIET. Mr. Martin! No indeed! I hope I know better now, than to care for Mr. Martin, or to be suspected of it. Please, dear Miss Woodhouse, have I not grounds for hope? I never would have presumed to think of it at first. You told me to observe him carefully and let his behavior be the rule of mine—and so I have. But now I seem to feel that I may deserve him.

EMMA. Harriet, I will only venture to declare, that Mr. Knightly is the last man in the world who would intentionally give any woman the idea of his feeling more for her than he really does.

(HARRIET embraces her then pulls back.)

HARRIET. I believe I hear Mr. Woodhouse coming...

EMMA. I shouldn't think...

HARRIET. I must go. I cannot compose myself and Mr. Woodhouse would be alarmed. *(Embraces EMMA again.)* My very dear Miss Woodhouse!

(HARRIET runs off. EMMA is alone.)

SNOW ANGEL

by David Lindsay-Abaire

Characters

EVA

FRIDA

Scene

Frida, the class outcast, works behind the counter at the local Pretzel Knot. On a break from her miserable job, she has yet another encounter with Eva, a strange and enigmatic girl she first met flailing about in a snowdrift in the woods.

(FRIDA writes in her journal.)

FRIDA. I'm gonna sprinkle rat poison on their pretzels and tell them it's powdered sugar. I can't wait to move away and mail a giant bomb back and level this stupid town.

(EVA appears. She's been listening.)

FRIDA. What are you looking at?

EVA. You're very angry.

FRIDA. Mind your own business, weirdo. Why aren't you making angels somewhere?

EVA. I'm finished with that.

FRIDA. Where'd you come from anyway?

EVA. I don't know. You shouldn't let those kids make you mad. They just think they're being funny.

FRIDA. Well they're not.

EVA. So tell them they hurt your feelings and maybe they'll quit.

FRIDA. They didn't hurt my feelings.

EVA. Alright.

FRIDA. And they wouldn't quit anyway. You don't even know them. Go away.

EVA. I like your name.

FRIDA. What?

EVA. Frida. It's a nice name.

FRIDA. You're nuts.

(Pause.)

I was named after Frida Kahlo. You know her?

EVA. No.

FRIDA. Of course not. She's a famous artist with one giant eyebrow across her forehead. Later in life she became a paraplegic. I relate to her.

EVA. Have you seen Whitestone?

FRIDA. Quit asking me that.

EVA. Sorry.

FRIDA. You're so annoying. What is it, a gas station or something?

EVA. No.

FRIDA. Maybe you're confusing it with the White Castle. The burger place?

EVA. It's a farm.

FRIDA. A farm?

EVA. The Whitestone Farm. It's where I live.

FRIDA. Oh. Not a lot of farms around here. Wait, you forget where you live?

EVA. No, I was looking for my little sister in the woods, but I couldn't find her, so I decided to go back home because maybe she was there, but now I don't know where it is. My home, I mean.

FRIDA. Do you have amnesia?

EVA. I don't know.

FRIDA. It happened during the blizzard?

EVA. The snow was up to my waist, but I saw something gray in the woods. I thought it was my sister's dress, but maybe it was just a rabbit. And I ran towards it, and the snow was getting deeper, but I kept running, and then a hole opened up under me. And there was snow all around me, and I was falling, but I was sleeping at the same time. And when I woke up, I was back in the woods, and it was quiet. And I made a snow angel, and then I saw you.

FRIDA. That's screwy. Are you on any kind of medication?

EVA. So you don't have any friends?

FRIDA. What?

EVA. There's nothing wrong with that. I didn't really have any either. I was at the farm all the time, so it was just me and the butter churn.

FRIDA. Whatever.

EVA. I'll be your friend if you help me find Whitestone.

FRIDA. I don't even know what you're talking about.

EVA. I need to go.

FRIDA. Hold on. I'm gonna call the police for you.

EVA. No, I have to go.

(EVA exits. FRIDA looks after her, perplexed.)

THE DISAPPEARANCE OF DANIEL HAND

by Dan O'Brien

Characters

SHANNON, a high school senior.

GIRL, homeless, 17.

Scene

Shannon, a young aspiring filmmaker, has gone to New York City in search of a classmate who recently went missing. At the end of a long, somewhat harrowing night, she meets a homeless girl in Grand Central Station. Also, Shannon's video camera was a gift from her estranged father.

Author Note

An entire line like this:

…

or

… ?

indicates a significant beat, perhaps played as a pause.

GIRL. Stuck?

SHANNON. What?

GIRL. I said, you stuck here for the night?

> *(She's sitting against the wall, a piece of cardboard beneath her, and another, smaller piece in front of her that reads something like: "I need money for a bus ticket home. Please help."*
>
> *A paper cup for change…)*

GIRL. You got any money?

SHANNON. No.

GIRL. Yes you do.

SHANNON. I'm sorry. —Excuse me—

> *(She starts to walk away.)*

GIRL. You do.

SHANNON. What:

GIRL. —I said you've got some money. Some change at least…

SHANNON. I don't have any money for you. I'm sorry.

(*She turns to leave again.*)

GIRL. You can't keep running away.

SHANNON. … ?

GIRL. (*She smiles.*) …Are you afraid?

SHANNON. Of you?

GIRL. …

SHANNON. Here's five dollars—

GIRL. You don't have to give me that much—

SHANNON. I want to—for your—bus.

(*She puts the money in her paper cup.*)

GIRL. You're afraid to touch me.

SHANNON. I didn't touch you—

GIRL. I know: you touched the cup. Barely. —You didn't want to touch the cup; with your hand.

SHANNON. —Why are you taking a bus?

GIRL. … ?

SHANNON. You're in a train station—

GIRL. Trains don't take me where I'm going.

SHANNON. …That sounds poetic…

GIRL. Does it?

SHANNON. Yeah. Like a song lyric.

GIRL. …

SHANNON. …

GIRL. —Buses are cheaper, that's all.

SHANNON. That's good to know…

GIRL. —What is?

SHANNON. That you're not lying. —Sometimes I see these signs and I think people are lying…

GIRL. Do you always think people are lying?

SHANNON. (*Shrugs.*) …

GIRL. People are frightened of me…
It upsets me. I'm dirty. I'm depressed. But mostly because I'm dirty, and asking for help…
People don't like to be asked for help. Why is that?

SHANNON. …

GIRL. How old am I?

SHANNON. I don't know.

GIRL. No—guess:

SHANNON. I don't know—

GIRL. Come on:

SHANNON. Twenty-two.

GIRL. Seventeen.

SHANNON. Me too!

GIRL. Just turned it.

SHANNON. —So did I—

GIRL. Yeah?

SHANNON. Yeah. In September?

GIRL. Wow. Cool… We must be the same sign…

SHANNON. …Are you making fun of me?

GIRL. *(Smiles.)* A little…

SHANNON. *(She smiles too.)* …

GIRL. You want to sit down?

SHANNON. *(She does.)* …Sure.

GIRL. …That your camera?

SHANNON. Uh-huh.

GIRL. Expensive…

SHANNON. Not really.

GIRL. How much did it cost you?

SHANNON. I got it—as a gift.

GIRL. Like a Christmas present? Or for your birthday?

SHANNON. For my birthday. From my dad.

GIRL. …That's cool…

SHANNON. Why are you here? You know: begging.

GIRL. I ran away; about a year ago…

SHANNON. Why?

GIRL. *(Shrugs.)* I didn't want to be home, I guess.

SHANNON. How'd you do it? —How'd you run away?

GIRL. *(Strongly:)* I don't want to talk about it—.

SHANNON. …

GIRL. …I left with my boyfriend…

SHANNON. …Is he here?

GIRL. In Seattle…

SHANNON. Is that where you're from?

GIRL. No.
…We're not together anymore.

SHANNON. …Do you ever want to go home?

GIRL. Never.

SHANNON. Why not?

GIRL. That's not an option for me…

SHANNON. If you're homeless—

GIRL. I can't—.
Okay? *(Quietly:)*
It's just not an option…

SHANNON. I don't think you should've done that.

GIRL. …

SHANNON. You shouldn't've run away from home: it's not fair.

GIRL. To who?

SHANNON. To the people you left behind.

GIRL. …You don't know why I left…

SHANNON. So?
Even if your parents were terrible—like they, I don't know, abused you—.
Don't you have any friends… ? Isn't there anyone who might miss you? —
You can't just give up on people. You can't just disappear.

GIRL. …I did…

SHANNON. …What do you do for money?

GIRL. Stuff…

SHANNON. Like what?

GIRL. Use your imagination.

SHANNON. …

GIRL. …

SHANNON. Here:

GIRL. What are you doing—?

SHANNON. *(Overlapping:)* I'm giving you my camera.

GIRL. *(She pushes it away.)* …

SHANNON. Take it: I don't want it anymore. I don't need it.

GIRL. —What do I need it for?

SHANNON. You can sell it. If you want. —Can you sell it?

GIRL. …

SHANNON. You can take the money. Go to Seattle.

GIRL. *(She smiles.)* Thanks…

SHANNON. …

GIRL. —I was going to steal it, you know.

SHANNON. … ?

GIRL. When you fell asleep, here, next to me: I was going to steal it from you…

> *(SHANNON places the camera in her hands.)*

SHANNON. I'm giving it to you now.

SCHOOLGIRL FIGURE

by Wendy MacLeod

Characters

RENEE, an anorexic high-school girl.

PATTY, her best friend, a bulimic high-school girl.

Scene

Monique, the reigning anorexic queen of the Carpenters, has just collapsed and been taken to the hospital. Fellow Carpenter Renee is anxious to get there before her rival Jeanine does, so that Monique might name her as official successor. But Patty insists on throwing up first, causing them to be caught in the "after-lunch rush hour" in the girls' bathroom.

Author Note

When dialogue appears in brackets, feel free to update the cultural reference.

(A school corridor. RENEE and PATTY stand in line outside the girls' bathroom door. There is the occasional flushing sound.)

RENEE. What's the hold up? How long does it take these girls to spew?

PATTY. It's the after-lunch rush hour.

RENEE. Why don't you just spew at the hospital? There won't be a line there.

PATTY. If I wait any longer, I'll digest.

RENEE. All this standing. I'm getting tired.

PATTY. You're tired because you don't eat enough.

RENEE. Don't eat enough?! I don't eat at all.

PATTY. What is your body supposed to live off of?

RENEE. I'm heavier than I look. If you saw me without my clothes...

PATTY. I see you without your clothes all the time. You weigh yourself naked four times a day.

RENEE. I'm trying to get an accurate reading.

PATTY. All I ever see is bones.

RENEE. You're sweet.

PATTY. It doesn't look good, Renee...

34

RENEE. And don't start on Marilyn Monroe again, whatever you do…

PATTY. She was a…

PATTY / RENEE. Size 12!

RENEE. I know. Marilyn Monroe was JELL-O on springs. It was a different, slothful time. This is the millennium. We can't be all post-war. Yo Princess Dianas! Finish and flush!

PATTY. You were a twelve before we came to this school…

RENEE. I was a large ten! I had glands.

PATTY. You didn't have glands, you were naturally a twelve.

RENEE. And what is so great about nature? Nature is a fiend. Ticks, tornados, and malaria are "natural." I mean, don't go all crunchy on me. I swear every day is Earth Day with you around.

PATTY. Just because I put my soda can in the recycling bin…

RENEE. It was *fanatical.* Come on, we've got to get to the hospital before Monique buys the farm.

PATTY. I can't miss sixth period, I have a Biology test.

RENEE. Would you stop? What a schoolgirl.

PATTY. Don't you think Monique dying is kind of sad?

RENEE. Why? Look at the Carpenter. She's famous.

PATTY. Yeah, but she was famous for doing something.

RENEE. Rainy Days and Mondays. Please.

PATTY. Monique's not gonna be famous. I mean she's the third one at this school alone.

RENEE. The first one was really sad. You remember Andrea's funeral? We all cried so much.

PATTY. *(Correcting the pronunciation:)* Andrea.

      (Toilet flush.)

RENEE. We have to get to the hospital before Jeanine.

PATTY. I don't know why you think Monique is gonna leave you for The Bradley.

RENEE. It's in the by-laws. In case of a tie the reigning Carpenter can choose her successor.

PATTY. Jeanine is her best friend. What makes you think she won't choose her?

RENEE. Solidarity. Jeanine isn't a true Carpenter. She's an obsessive exerciser. She went crazy when she couldn't figure out how to exercise her head.

PATTY. Is that why she talks that way?

RENEE. Yeah. Too much group therapy.

PATTY. Can't we go to the hospital *after* school?

RENEE. I have to be there for Monique now. In her hour of need.

PATTY. As if.

RENEE. Don't be all… I can be nice.

PATTY. When?

RENEE. I also want to be there for The Bradley. What, he doesn't deserve comfort just cause he's gorgeous?

PATTY. He doesn't even know you.

RENEE. That can only help.

PATTY. The Bradley must be getting tired of his girlfriends croaking.

RENEE. It's every man's fantasy. Rotating women without ever having to break up. Dead girlfriends are the ultimate pick-up line. Who's going to say no to a guy with a dead girlfriend?

PATTY. Have you ever talked to him?

RENEE. Why?

PATTY. Is he smart?

RENEE. Smart?

PATTY. I mean, what's he like?

RENEE. *(Impatient:)* He's The Bradley.

PATTY. You know what Tricia said? She said maybe The Bradley isn't that great.

RENEE. Just because there's no chance in hell for that fat little hen… After the monthly weigh-in, Tricia's gone!

PATTY. They'll really send her away?

RENEE. Ten and over. Gone! They divvy up her clothes. Talk about a tent sale.

PATTY. Who made up the by-laws? Where did they come from?

RENEE. Who knows? My mother lived on Melba Toast. Her Nana bound her breasts. They've always been there. Like celery and Seconal. Speaking of by-laws, Patty, you're still looking a little double-digit and you know the rules. Beyond an eight is beyond the pale.

PATTY. All I've got to do is balance out my binges and purges.

RENEE. Well you're on probation. You've got a week to lose five pounds. Err on the side of purge.

> *(RENEE shoves PATTY through the door for her turn and follows her in. Loud flush.)*

DOROTHY AND ALICE

by Itamar Moses

Characters

DOROTHY, a young girl, with brown hair.

ALICE, another young girl, with blonde hair.

Scene

An elementary school playground, lunchtime. Two seemingly ordinary young girls meet and eat lunch together.

> *(ALICE sits on a bench with a brown-bag lunch. She takes items out of her bag and sets them on the bench next to her: a slice of cake, a small flask filled with colorful liquid. Sounds of children laughing and playing are distantly audible. A second girl, DOROTHY, approaches. She, too, has a brown-bag lunch.)*
>
> *(DOROTHY stares at ALICE for a few moments. A wind rustles them both, and ALICE looks up, suddenly.)*

ALICE. Oh! Hello.

DOROTHY. Hi. *(Pause.)* Do you…?

ALICE. What?

DOROTHY. Do you mind if I eat with you?

ALICE. Oh! Not at all! Sit, sit. Sit.

DOROTHY. *(She does so, relieved:)* Thank you. I hate not having anyone to eat with. It makes me feel very—

ALICE. I know.

DOROTHY. Sometimes, I like to eat by myself, anyway. But I'd just some-one to ask. So I have the choice.

ALICE. I know.

DOROTHY. But nobody does.

ALICE. *(Beat.)* Do you want to eat alone?

DOROTHY. What? Oh, no. Today I asked because I really want someone to eat with.

ALICE. I'm Alice.

DOROTHY. I know.

ALICE. You're Dorothy, right?

DOROTHY. *(Pleased:)* Yes!

ALICE. I pay attention during roll call. I pay attention to everything. My big sister thinks I'm absent-minded but I'm very observant is the truth.

DOROTHY. Most people don't know my name, because—

ALICE. You just moved here.

DOROTHY. That's right! You're very—

ALICE. I'm very observant. Also, the first day you were in class you gave a speech: "My name is Dorothy. And I just moved here."

DOROTHY. From Kansas.

ALICE. I know. *(Pause.)* I'd love to visit Kansas.

DOROTHY. What for? It's a very boring place.

ALICE. No, I don't think so. I think it's exciting.

DOROTHY. But you've never been there.

ALICE. Exactly!

DOROTHY. What?

ALICE. Even the *word* is exciting. Kansas! Kaaaan-sas! It sounds so strange and wonderful, doesn't it?

DOROTHY. *(Pause.)* No.

ALICE. It does!

DOROTHY. No. I lived there. There's nothing.

ALICE. Why did you move away?

DOROTHY. There were…problems with the weather.

ALICE. Well, it was silly to move here.

DOROTHY. What do you mean? This place is much more exciting than Kansas.

ALICE. Maybe. But now that you're here, it will just be the place that you are, which is never as exciting as places you haven't been, but might go to.

DOROTHY. I know what you mean.

ALICE. No, I don't think you do.

DOROTHY. No, I think I know what you mean better even that you do.

ALICE. I really don't think that's possible.

DOROTHY. Well, I guess we'll just see.

ALICE. Yes, I guess we will.

(Pause.)

DOROTHY. That's a pretty weird lunch you've got.

ALICE. What do you mean?

DOROTHY. Well, it's just cake, and a drink. That's not very healthy. Don't your parents want to make sure you eat right?

ALICE. Oh, I didn't get these from my parents.

DOROTHY. Really? Then who made you these thoughtful notes?

(DOROTHY turns the food so that we can see there are notes on ALICE's lunch. The cake says "EAT ME" and the potion says "DRINK ME.")

ALICE. I don't know. *(Pause. She considers the cake.)* Do you ever feel like you're growing up too fast?

DOROTHY. Of course. All the time.

ALICE. Me too. I'm afraid of getting so big that I can't even fit in *(side of)*—

DOROTHY. Tell me about it. Fitting in is so hard, what with moving, and everything. I feel so awkward all the time, like I'm saying or doing something wrong.

ALICE. What? Oh, no, I meant… Literally. Changing…physically…

DOROTHY. *(Crosses her arms.)* Oh. Yeah. That makes me feel awkward too.

ALICE. *(Impressed:)* You know what I'm talking about?

DOROTHY. Of course. It happens to all of us, doesn't it?

ALICE. Are you sure?

DOROTHY. Oh, yes!

ALICE. I don't *think* so. Falling, all alone, down a dark hole…?

DOROTHY. It can feel like that. But it happens to everybody. Even animals. That's how I learned about it. Watching animals on my farm.

ALICE. You had a farm?

DOROTHY. Yes.

ALICE. I'd love to visit a farm!

DOROTHY. Why? Farms aren't very exciting.

ALICE. Of course they are! Listen: Faaarm. Faaaarm. What a wonderful word! It even has the word "Far" *in it.* That's what makes it sound so far away and exciting.

DOROTHY. It doesn't matter what other words are in it. You can be right on top of a farm, and it would still have the word "far" in it.

ALICE. No, I think then it would be a Nearm.

DOROTHY. You're very silly about words.

ALICE. I'm sorry.

DOROTHY. No, I like it.

ALICE. Really? You should hear me rhyme!

DOROTHY. I'd love to! *(Pause.)* Those are things they don't let you do so much when you grow up.

ALICE. I know.

DOROTHY. The years just start to slip away, swallowed up by—

ALICE. Giant monsters.

DOROTHY. *(Beat.)* I was going to say: "Responsibility."

ALICE. Oh.

DOROTHY. My Aunt and Uncle are always talking about "responsibility." *(Beat.)* What were you thinking of?

ALICE. The Jabberwock.

DOROTHY. What's that?

ALICE. Responsibility also. More or less.

DOROTHY. Sometimes, I just wish there was a magic potion I could use that would make me small forever.

> *(ALICE offers DOROTHY her drink. DOROTHY doesn't pick up that this is a direct response to her wish, and declines:)*

DOROTHY. Oh, no, thank you. I have my own drink.

> *(DOROTHY takes a large bucket of water out of her bag.)*

ALICE. What is that?

DOROTHY. Just water.

ALICE. Why so much of it?

DOROTHY. I always like to have a lot of it with me. You never know when you might need it, for self-defense.

ALICE. I know what you mean.

DOROTHY. You do?

ALICE. One time, Billy Thomason wouldn't leave me alone. He was chasing me all day. And then the teacher sprayed him with water and said, "Cool off." And he did.

DOROTHY. Why was he chasing you?

ALICE. I don't know.

DOROTHY. It was probably because you're changing physically.

ALICE. I hate boys. They're completely mad.

DOROTHY. No!

ALICE. They're heartless, brainless, cowardly, dogs.

DOROTHY. No! *(Beat.)* Well, yes. But not usually all four at once. And, even so, they're very dependable companions.

　　　　(Pause.)

ALICE. What kinds of problems with the weather?

DOROTHY. What?

ALICE. You said you left Kansas because of problems with the weather.

DOROTHY. Oh. Do you ever feel like you've been swept up in a great wind, and spun around, and flown through the air, and then dropped down somewhere completely unfamiliar and strange and frightening and even dangerous?

ALICE. That must be what it feels like to move.

DOROTHY. That's also what it feels like to move.

ALICE. Oh. I see.

DOROTHY. You do understand.

ALICE. Yes. Oh yes.

DOROTHY. Tell me.

　　　　(Something shifts. A string is plucked, somewhere. They each look out, as though in a trance, and speak slowly.)

ALICE. You were told to stay put, but you saw him, and chased him—

DOROTHY. Your small furry friend, kidnapped, pleading, his bark—

ALICE. Furry, yes, but huge, white, and his lateness disgraced him—

DOROTHY. You caught him—

ALICE. —no, lost him—

DOROTHY. —and then came the dark.

ALICE. And you found yourself falling and falling—

DOROTHY. No, rising, first.

ALICE. Clocks on the walls—

DOROTHY. —ripped away, as you passed.

ALICE. And then, wondering whether you'd weathered the worst—

DOROTHY. You descended—

ALICE. —so slowly—

DOROTHY. No, terribly fast.

ALICE. And you're there.

DOROTHY. But where?

ALICE. Wonderland?

DOROTHY. Oz?

ALICE. Brigadoon?

DOROTHY. Shangri-La?

ALICE. Lilliput?

DOROTHY. Narnia?

ALICE. Atlantis?

DOROTHY. And you'd wished for so long—

ALICE. —every bright afternoon—

DOROTHY. —every night, for adventures like this.

(Pause. They look at each other.)

ALICE. But now that you're there, free to play—

DOROTHY. —free to roam.

ALICE. You have a new wish.

DOROTHY. Yes, that's true.

ALICE. Your wish is for home.

DOROTHY. To find home.

ALICE. To go home.

GOVERNING ALICE

C. Denby Swanson

Characters

ALICE

IZZY, her sister.

Scene

Punk sister Alice and goody-goody sister Izzy meet up at the convenience store crime scene where their brother, the high school valedictorian, was killed in the course of committing a robbery.

> *(Convenience Store.*
>
> *ALICE stands outside, by the solid brick wall, contemplating where to aim her graffiti. IZZY enters.)*

IZZY. What are you doing here?

ALICE. Nothing.

IZZY. Yeah? Gosh, that's funny. Me too.

ALICE. Don't try it, Izzy, you're too much of a nerd.

> *(ALICE shakes the can.)*

IZZY. Is that spray paint?

> *(ALICE just looks at her.)*

IZZY. What are you gonna do with it?

ALICE. I guess I'm going to spray. Paint.

> *(Pause.)*

IZZY. You left so early this morning. I thought—I don't know what I thought. And Mom couldn't take me to school, so I walked. I walked all the way here.

ALICE. You win a prize.

IZZY. Was this where—?

ALICE. That's what the police tape indicated.

IZZY. I don't think you're supposed to take that stuff down.

> *(They look at the pile that ALICE has dismantled.)*

ALICE. Have some if you want.

IZZY. Okay.

(IZZY shyly takes a section of it and stuffs it in her backpack.)

ALICE. You can do all kinds of things now, Ethan's not around to—whatever. Whole new world.

IZZY. Funny, this was the one thing he didn't do exactly right.

(Pause.)

ALICE. Yeah.

IZZY. If they say he did it—

ALICE. That's the question?

IZZY. I mean, he did it.

ALICE. Yes.

(Pause.)

IZZY. I just don't know anymore.

ALICE. What don't you know?

IZZY. Well, I guess, like, how we—still love him.

ALICE. How could you possibly not know that?

IZZY. Alice—

ALICE. How could you possibly not know?

IZZY. They said—

ALICE. "How do we still love him?"

IZZY. You didn't look up to him like I did.

ALICE. Has this made you stupid?

IZZY. Alice, don't be mean—

ALICE. He was my brother, too.

IZZY. But he robbed people. He stole money—

ALICE. Yes.

IZZY. He made everybody think he was good.

ALICE. Don't you?

IZZY. What.

ALICE. Miss Do Everything Right. Miss Predictable. Miss Follow the Directions.

IZZY. I don't lie like that.

ALICE. Who finished your chemistry project last month?

> *(Pause.)*

IZZY. That's not—

ALICE. Right.

IZZY. You're better at chemistry than me.

ALICE. I had to take it twice. I've memorized the answers.

> *(Pause.)*

IZZY. So—

ALICE. So nothing. So I don't know. About Ethan. Alright?

> *(IZZY turns to leave. She comes back.)*

IZZY. Mom said to tell everybody that he died in an accident.

ALICE. Yeah.

> *(ALICE shakes the spray paint again. She turns her can to the wall and presses down on the nozzle.)*

THE BLUEBERRY HILL ACCORD

by Daryl Watson

Characters

HANNAH

LINDSAY

Scene

Lindsay and Hannah have been best friends since the third grade. While eating at their favorite diner, Lindsay announces that it's time for them to break up so that they can move on and meet other people. Devastated, Hannah is about to walk out on her former friend, but Lindsay stops her. There's still one last thing that needs to be taken care of...

(Lights up on the Blueberry Hill diner. High school students HANNAH and LINDSAY are sitting across from each other in a booth.)

LINDSAY. Before we leave here today... There's a few things I'd like to get in writing.

(LINDSAY leans over, pulls her book bag up from the floor, and opens it. She removes several pieces of paper from the bag and sets them on the table. HANNAH stares at her in disbelief.)

LINDSAY. I've compiled some notes here... They're more bullet points, actually... I was thinking we could go over them and both sign at the bottom—

HANNAH. Is this a joke?

LINDSAY. Well... No...

HANNAH. I'm not signing anything.

LINDSAY. But—

HANNAH. NO! This is stupid.

LINDSAY. I feel this is the best—

HANNAH. I don't give a rat's behind what you feel.

(HANNAH rises again.)

LINDSAY. LOOK, I KNOW THINGS ABOUT YOU!

HANNAH. Are you threatening me?

LINDSAY. No! You know things about me too. Okay!? So it's in both of our best interests to settle this on paper.

(*A beat.*)

HANNAH. You're serious.

LINDSAY. Yes.

HANNAH. You really wanna do this.

LINDSAY. Yes.

HANNAH. You wanna add yet another layer of insanity to this whole thing.

LINDSAY. Well, I wouldn't—

HANNAH. No, no, no! You wanna do it, let's do it!

(*HANNAH sits down and grabs the papers, flipping through them.*)

HANNAH. First of all, I want all my stuff back from you.

LINDSAY. Right.

HANNAH. My Norah Jones CD...

LINDSAY. My copy of *Pride and Prejudice.*

HANNAH. My green top. My Magic 8-ball.

LINDSAY. You gave me the Magic 8-ball.

HANNAH. I lent you the 8-ball. You just never gave it back.

LINDSAY. You never asked for it. I've had it for three years.

HANNAH. Better late than never.

LINDSAY. Fine. And just so we're clear, I don't want you to say anything about me to other people.

HANNAH. Fine. And you better not say anything about me either.

LINDSAY. Fine.

HANNAH. And you know what? I don't want you telling the Joey Feinberg story anymore.

LINDSAY. WHAT? Why?

HANNAH. Because it's my story.

LINDSAY. But I always tell that story! It's a good story!

HANNAH. It's a great story! And you butcher it every time you tell it.

LINDSAY. I do not.

HANNAH. Lindsay, you could find a lottery ticket on the street, win a million dollars, get kidnapped by Columbian drug lords and held for ransom, go on *Oprah* to tell the whole world about it…and you'd still make it the most boring, yawn-inducing story ever. You have a knack for it.

LINDSAY. That's so mean!

HANNAH. It's the truth. I only let you tell the Joey Feinberg story because you're my friend. But if we're not friends anymore, you can't tell the story.

LINDSAY. Well, then, you can't tell the Lake Mead story.

HANNAH. What sense does that make?

LINDSAY. If I can't tell the Joey Feinberg story, you can't tell the Lake Mead story.

HANNAH. Excuse me! The Joey Feinberg story happened to me and Joey Feinberg. It's my story.

LINDSAY. And the Lake Mead story happened to both you *and* me. It's fifty percent mine, by rights, and I'm saying I don't want you telling it.

HANNAH. Fifty percent of it is mine too!

LINDSAY. Well, you can tell your fifty percent of it.

HANNAH. This is ridiculous.

LINDSAY. I'm serious. You can only talk about the stuff that happened to you. Leave me out of it.

HANNAH. Fine.

LINDSAY. And you can't tell anybody what I told you about my parents.

HANNAH. Okay.

LINDSAY. Promise me.

HANNAH. I promise. I'm writing it down. See? And you can't tell anybody about the time I got my period during that softball game.

LINDSAY. I thought everybody knew that.

HANNAH. Everyone thinks it was Jackie.

LINDSAY. Nuh-uh!

HANNAH. Why do you think they call her "Jackie Swab-inson?"

LINDSAY. Gross! That's awful!

HANNAH. Whatever. It's payback from when she told everybody I had mono, when I so didn't.

LINDSAY. I guess.

HANNAH. You guess right. She's a ho.

LINDSAY. Did you know she went after Tommy Marth, even after she knew I liked him?

HANNAH. 'Cause she's *like* that. I told you not to tell her you wanted him. But, for the record, I can date Tommy now.

LINDSAY. WHAT?

HANNAH. Once we sign this, all's fair.

LINDSAY. So does that mean I can date Adam?

HANNAH. Yeah. Sure. Whatever. I don't care.

LINDSAY. All right.

HANNAH. You can't tell anybody I'm seeing a therapist.

LINDSAY. You can't tell anybody *I'm* seeing a therapist. And you can't tell anybody I kissed Rachel Bumgardner at that party.

HANNAH. YOU KISSED RACHEL BUMGARDNER???

LINDSAY. Wait, you didn't know!?

HANNAH. NO!

LINDSAY. Oh my God. I cannot believe I just told you that.

HANNAH. So what happened? You *have* to tell me.

LINDSAY. It was so crazy…

> (*LINDSAY stops herself. A long beat.*)

I can't think of anything else to put down.

HANNAH. Actually… I have one more thing.

LINDSAY. What?

HANNAH. Neither of us can eat here. Ever.

LINDSAY. No way.

HANNAH. We can't, or I won't sign.

LINDSAY. Why?

HANNAH. Because Blueberry Hill is our spot! This is our place. This is where I told you about losing my virginity—

LINDSAY. Shhh!

HANNAH. …and you told me about you losing yours!

LINDSAY. SHHH!

HANNAH. We've stayed up late studying here, we've had all the big talks here: guys, religion, college, everything. It's holy ground. I don't care who you pick for your "really good friend," but you better not bring her here.

LINDSAY. I don't know…

HANNAH. Am I wrong? Doesn't that history mean anything to you?

LINDSAY. No, it does. I just...

HANNAH. What?

LINDSAY. I don't know! This is hard!

HANNAH. Well... I don't know what to tell you. I would have been perfectly happy if you'd just given me the silent treatment for eight months and talked about me behind my back while I went crazy trying to figure out what happened. That's how normal people end friendships. You're the one that wanted to turn it into the Geneva Convention.

LINDSAY. Okay.

HANNAH. So we're agreed? Blueberry Hill's off limits?

LINDSAY. Yeah.

HANNAH. Okay.

(A beat.)

So where should I sign?

LINDSAY. Well, we can't sign it like this.

HANNAH. Why not?

LINDSAY. It's all scribbles. It should be typed up in legalese, so that it at least looks legible.

(A beat.)

HANNAH. So who's going to do that?

LINDSAY. I guess I will.

(A beat.)

HANNAH. So in the meantime... Verbal agreement?

LINDSAY. I don't trust those. No one ever agrees on what was actually agreed upon. That's why you get things in writing. I mean... I'm willing to wait if you are.

HANNAH. I guess.

LINDSAY. At least until I get this typed up.

HANNAH. Right.

LINDSAY. You know?

HANNAH. Okay.

(A beat.)

Wait... I'm confused. So are we still friends?

LINDSAY. Well... I mean, until we sign this, technically, yeah. We are.

(A beat.)

HANNAH. Does that mean you're still coming over this weekend?

LINDSAY. Oh…

HANNAH. Because I'm just going to be hanging out, so… If you don't think you'll be done by then…

LINDSAY. We'll see. I got a lot of homework and rehearsal, so maybe I won't get to it. I don't know.

HANNAH. Or if you do finish it, you can bring it over, we can hang out, and then we'll sign it before you leave.

LINDSAY. Okay.

HANNAH. Whatever. We'll see what happens.

LINDSAY. Yeah.

(A long beat.)

HANNAH. *Rachel Bumgardner???*

LINDSAY. Okay, first of all, I was trashed beyond reason…

(As LINDSAY ad-libs the story, the lights fade to black.)

Scenes for Two Men

11 VARIATIONS ON FRIAR JOHN'S FAILURE

by Yuri Baranovsky

Characters

FRIAR JOHN

TOM SAWYER

Scene

In *Romeo and Juliet*, Friar John is charged to deliver a letter to Romeo telling him of Juliet's false demise. The Friar is supposedly waylaid by a break out of plague—but what is the real reason? In this variation, instead of plague, Friar John bumps into a young boy named Tom Sawyer, who offers him what sounds like a very fair trade…

> *(FRIAR JOHN enters, walking swiftly from stage right, and off, to stage left. A teenager sits near a fence, and paints it quietly on the opposite side of the stage. FRIAR JOHN slowly backs up, and looks at TOM SAWYER with curiosity.)*

FRIAR JOHN. Good day, sire. What doest thou 'pon this road?

TOM SAWYER. Ain't it obvious, mister?

FRIAR JOHN. Nay, nay, 'tisn't.

> *(TOM ignores him, continues painting.)*

FRIAR JOHN. I shall say it again, sire, for thou didst hear me not. Nay, I do not understand thine activity.

TOM SAWYER. I'm whitewashin' this 'ere fence, mister.

FRIAR JOHN. Whitewashing? Thou dost speak of things which I have yet to hear, art thou mad or simply dumb?

TOM SAWYER. You ain't from 'round here, are ye?

FRIAR JOHN. I hail from Verona.

TOM SAWYER. Long way away from home then.

FRIAR JOHN. Aye. The duties of a Friar do often take him places that only God has seen!

TOM SAWYER. And the people livin' in those places.

FRIAR JOHN. Pardon?

TOM SAWYER. God, and the people livin' in those places.

(There is a pause; they stare at each other.)

FRIAR JOHN. Right.

(There is more silence. TOM shrugs, and begins to paint the fence again. FRIAR JOHN watches him curiously.)

FRIAR JOHN. An interesting activity, that. *(Pause.)* One I have yet to attempt in mine busy life, busied as I am with chores, blessings…baptizing stuff. *(Pause.)* I wonder if such a skill is taught in Verona, or if thou didst acquire it in thy short youth, and didst develop such a knack that thou dost do so for a living.

TOM SAWYER. *(Looks up at him:)* Are you still talkin'? Why, I ain't even notice ye, so involved am I in th'fence. Th'fence is fun. I love this fence. If I was older, an' my aunt let me, I'd marry it.

FRIAR JOHN. The fence?

TOM SAWYER. Yeah.

FRIAR JOHN. Yes…well… I would be on my way, then. I shall deliver this letter thusly and return to my duties—I can see thou'rt the busy lad, working as you are. Adieu. *(Begins to walk off.)*

TOM SAWYER. Work? Whattaya call work?

FRIAR JOHN. Why, good sir, do not you, with thy well-worn practitioner's hand know the likes of work? *(Points at the fence:)* That, sir, is work!

TOM SAWYER. Well, maybe it is. And maybe it ain't. You'll never know though, 'cause you ain't ever gonna do it. *(Suddenly very excited:)* Oh!

FRIAR JOHN. What!

TOM SAWYER. Didja see that?!

FRIAR JOHN. Nay, what?!

TOM SAWYER. Aw. Nevermind. Ya gotta be paintin' t'see it. It was real neat though.

FRIAR JOHN. *(Looks at him skeptically:)* Surely, sir, you do not speak of liking such a task! Verily, 'tis one of little diversity, and indeed, a matter of much tedium.

TOM SAWYER. Liking it? How many days does a boy jus' get to white-wash a fence? Normally, you'd say, what, three? four days? But you'd be wrong. It's one. Just one.

FRIAR JOHN. *(Watches TOM silently.)* Good sir, what would it take thee to allow me feel of such a fence, and indeed, perhaps spend a bit doing thine own task?

TOM SAWYER. Mm. I dunno if I can let ye do that. M'aunt's particular 'bout her fence. 'Specially 'bout the people who do it. See, I got a practiced hand, and one outta a thousand others can do it the way she wants it t'be done. And frankly, we don't often trust weird speakin' folks from…Veroner?

FRIAR JOHN. Dear sir, how thou dost tease me with thy cruel words. It is as if thou didst unleash thy very blade 'pon my heart, and struck me thus— an old man Friar—'pon my dignity. Surely, you would allow me to prove that I am capable of such a task as you yourself perform forthwith!

TOM SAWYER. Mm. It'll cost ye…

FRIAR JOHN. This robe? I'd gladly—

TOM SAWYER. Nah. Nah.

FRIAR JOHN. My shoes, here, here—

TOM SAWYER. Nah! No shoes.

FRIAR JOHN. *(Sighs.)* My hair then, aye. 'Twill be but a moment. *(Takes out a knife and puts it against hair.)*

TOM SAWYER. Nah! Nah. I just want th'letter.

FRIAR JOHN. Oh, sir, I cannot—

TOM SAWYER. Then no deal.

FRIAR JOHN. How unfairly the fates do rule this land! Come, sir. Another offer?

TOM SAWYER. Letter, or you ain't got a deal.

FRIAR JOHN. Alack, alack, I am undone! Here, sire. Take it. Take it. Take it!

> *(FRIAR JOHN hands TOM the letter, TOM hands FRIAR JOHN the paintbrush.)*

TOM SAWYER. Top o' the morn t'ye then. *(Exits.)*

> *(FRIAR JOHN kneels next to fence, begins painting. A moment passes —to audience:)*

FRIAR JOHN. This isn't so fun. *(Pauses, in thought.)* Methinks a piece of particularly horrid tomfoolery hath befallen me. I've been made a tomfool!

> *(Sighs, and continues working.)*

Woe is me.

DOWN CAME THE RAIN

by Burgess Clark

Characters

MICHAEL, 18. Softly rugged. Medium build. A young man of simple good looks, he is very tolerant—yet can be rather cruel at times. Despite all the turmoil he loves Brucie deeply.

BRUCIE, 14. Michael's brother. Small; frail. Considered mentally "slow" since birth. He depends on Michael for everything, holding simple love and admiration for him.

Scene

Michael and Brucie are in the midst of a brotherly camping trip. Brucie's endless series of questions, especially regarding their dead mother, is beginning to tip Michael's patience to the breaking point.

> *(A remote campsite in fall. It is early evening. A tent dominates the upper portion of the stage. A small circle of stones representing a fire ring is in the lower section. Otherwise, requirements are few. Several camping articles are scattered around the site, such as a cooler, a spread-out sleeping bag, and so on. Small pieces of trash give a general feeling of carelessness about the space.)*
>
> *(The stage is empty as the lights slowly rise. A bird calls in the far-off distance. Crickets and other general nature noises prevail.)*
>
> *(The two sit for a moment.)*

BRUCIE. What did Mama look like?

MICHAEL. I told you. I don't remember.

BRUCIE. You don't remember anything about her?

MICHAEL. I didn't say that.

BRUCIE. You do remember something about her?

> *(MICHAEL shrugs.)*

Tell me, Mickey. What do you remember?

MICHAEL. *(Rising:)* Naw…

BRUCIE. Please?

MICHAEL. It's not very much, anyway. *(Pause.)* Well, I remember when she told me that she was going to have a baby.

BRUCIE. What baby was she going to have?

MICHAEL. You.

BRUCIE. Me?

MICHAEL. Yeah. I remember when she told me she was going to have you. I was lying in my bed, but I wasn't asleep. It was very dark in my room, but I could see the light in the hallway shining underneath my door. Suddenly, she came in and I remember seeing her silhouette in the door frame. She said very softly, "Are you asleep, Michael?" *(Pause.)* I said that I wasn't, so she came into my room and sat on the edge of my bed. She felt my forehead for fever, asked me if I felt all right. I said I was wondering what all the relatives were so excited about. She laughed and said that she had a big surprise for me. She said, "You're going to have a baby brother or sister to play with in a few months…" She said I could help her take care of it. She said she would really need my help. Then she bent down and kissed me and told me to go to sleep. I was so happy. She was so happy. Everybody was so happy…

BRUCIE. Is that what you remember, brother Michael? What did she look like?

MICHAEL. I told you. I don't know.

BRUCIE. But—

MICHAEL. It was dark. All I can remember is what she said. Her voice was so soft, Brucie—so soft. She was so beautiful…

> *(He removes the photo from his pocket.)*

BRUCIE. Can I see?

MICHAEL. What?

BRUCIE. Can I see what you have?

> *(MICHAEL pauses uncertainly.)*

Please?

MICHAEL. All right. *(Handing it to BRUCIE:)* Here. Be *careful.*

BRUCIE. Is that her?

MICHAEL. Yes, that's her.

BRUCIE. She was pretty.

MICHAEL. Yes. She was.

> *(MICHAEL goes to the cooler for another beer.)*

BRUCIE. I don't remember anything at all. I guess that's because I was so small when she died, huh?

> *(As MICHAEL's back is turned, BRUCIE shuffles the photograph in among his baseball cards.)*

Do you remember our mother's funeral?

MICHAEL. No. I didn't go. I stayed with Aunt Trudy.

BRUCIE. Did I go?

MICHAEL. You were still in the hospital.

BRUCIE. Did our mother die in the hospital?

MICHAEL. Yes, she died the morning after you were born.

BRUCIE. But I didn't kill her.

MICHAEL. No.

BRUCIE. And she was sick.

MICHAEL. Yes. Very sick. Very, very sick…

> *(MICHAEL turns and sees BRUCIE's treatment of the photo.)*

BRUCIE!

BRUCIE. What…?

MICHAEL. *(Snatching the cards from him:)* You never learn…

BRUCIE. Hey! Those are my cards!

> *(MICHAEL retrieves the photo. He scatters the cards across the ground, moving away.)*

Mickey?

> *(There is silence. BRUCIE begins to gather up the cards.)*

You know what else I think about while you're at school, brother Michael? Do you know what else I think?

MICHAEL. No. What else do you think, Brucie.

BRUCIE. I think about what's gonna happen.

MICHAEL. You do. What's going to happen.

BRUCIE. This is after—what I think about. It's after.

MICHAEL. It's after what?

BRUCIE. It's after we leave Daddy.

MICHAEL. What do you mean, "after *we* leave Daddy?"

BRUCIE. When we go away. You know—when we go away on our own.

MICHAEL. Go where?

BRUCIE. I don't know. But it's just gonna be you and me, Mickey—just you and me. And we're gonna be in a cave.

MICHAEL. A cave?!

BRUCIE. *(Beaming:)* Uh huh. A cave. Just like Batman and Robin. And we'll have this neat car with guns and a 'jector seat and stuff—and…and… you won't have to go to school anymore, because you'll be so smart, you won't have anything else to learn. And you'll take care of me—forever and ever.

MICHAEL. What about Dad?

BRUCIE. Oh. Well he can still visit. But most of the time it's gonna be just you and me—all alone in the cave. And you'll take care of me—

MICHAEL. —And I'll take care of you—

BRUCIE. —forever and ever. And we'll be happy. Forever and ever.

MICHAEL. Sure, Brucie.

BRUCIE. I can't wait. It'll be Christmas day for everyday, too. We'll just give each other presents. *(Pause.)* Will you sing me the song, now?

MICHAEL. Maybe later.

BRUCIE. And you're going to sing me the song whenever I want.

MICHAEL. That's a real nice story, Brucie.

BRUCIE. And it's gonna happen, too.

MICHAEL. How do you know?

BRUCIE. I just know, that's all. We'll always be together.

> *(BRUCIE resumes playing about the campsite. MICHAEL remains stationary, lost in his thoughts.)*

Brother Michael, I—

MICHAEL. *(Snaps:)* Don't call me that anymore, okay?!

BRUCIE. What.

MICHAEL. Don't call me *that* anymore. "Brother."

BRUCIE. But, that's what you are—

MICHAEL. I know. Just don't say it anymore, okay? *(Pause.)* That's kid stuff, Brucie. That's what you've called me ever since you could talk. My name is Michael. *Just* Michael. Call me Michael.

BRUCIE. *(Slowly:)* I do, sometimes.

MICHAEL. I know that you do. Call me that all the time from now on.

BRUCIE. Can I still call you Mickey?

MICHAEL. Sure.

BRUCIE. *(Quietly:)* I love you, Mickey.

MICHAEL. Thanks, Brucie.

> *(There is another break in the conversation. BRUCIE watches MICHAEL carefully.)*

BRUCIE. *(Suddenly:)* Do you remember when I was homed?

MICHAEL. *(Sighs:)* Yes.

BRUCIE. Tell me about that please.

MICHAEL. What do you mean?

BRUCIE. What did I look like?

MICHAEL. *(Smiles:)* God—you were ugly.

BRUCIE. I was not!

MICHAEL. You were too! *All* babies are ugly when they're first born, no matter what anybody says. I was so disappointed.

BRUCIE. You were?

MICHAEL. *(Laughing:)* Yeah. I was picturing this little boy that I could play with. You were just this scrawny, puny, bawling brat.

BRUCIE. But I grew up, huh?

MICHAEL. Yeah. You grew up.

BRUCIE. I cried a lot when I was a baby.

MICHAEL. All the time. I was the one who started to sing to you to get you to sleep.

BRUCIE. The song?! Was it the song?!

MICHAEL. Yes, it was that goddamned song. It was the only way to get you to shut up. Mrs. Schmidt caught me one day trying to stuff a washcloth into your mouth just to stop your goddamned screaming.

> *(They both laugh.)*

BRUCIE. Really?

MICHAEL. And you wore diapers until you were almost six…

> *(BRUCIE stops laughing.)*

BRUCIE. *(Indignantly:)* I did not!

MICHAEL. Sorry little brother, but I'm afraid you did.

BRUCIE. That's a lie!

MICHAEL. *(Playing it up:)* Believe me, I wouldn't lie about a thing like that.

BRUCIE. It's…it's…it's a *goddamned* lie!

MICHAEL. Ask Dad if you don't believe me.

BRUCIE. I will!

MICHAEL. Fine! See what he says. That's what Mrs. Schmidt was there for—to change your dirty diapers.

BRUCIE. No! It didn't happen!

MICHAEL. *(Baiting:)* I used to yell, "Mrs. Schmidt! Mrs. Schmidt! Brucie crapped his pants again!"

BRUCIE. *(Enraged:)* YOU'RE A GODDAMNED LIAR!

> *(BRUCIE pounces on MICHAEL, beating on him. For the first few swings, MICHAEL simply laughs. The blows get harder: MICHAEL holds BRUCIE away.)*

MICHAEL. Stop it! Brucie! Goddamn it! Stop it!

BRUCIE. It's a goddamned lie!

MICHAEL. Stop it, do you hear me?!

> *(Suddenly BRUCIE launches one well placed blow to the head. They stop. BRUCIE backs away. MICHAEL moves towards him.)*

BRUCIE. Michael—I'm sorry—

> *(MICHAEL slaps BRUCIE. BRUCIE screams in pain and begins to cry.)*

MICHAEL. Shut up, now! Shut the hell up! You deserved that, you little retarded shit!

> *(BRUCIE continues to wail—louder. MICHAEL grabs him by the shoulders, shaking him.)*

Shut up, Brucie! BRUCIE, STOP IT! SHUT UP!

> *(He strikes BRUCIE again. A frenzy begins, where MICHAEL loses control. He knocks BRUCIE to the ground.)*

STOP IT! STOP SCREAMING, BRUCIE! STOP SCREAMING…!

> *(MICHAEL kicks BRUCIE violently in the stomach. Suddenly MICHAEL stops. He retreats to the far side of the area, desperately trying to calm himself. He runs back to BRUCIE, who continues to cry.)*

Brucie…?

(He touches the boy. BRUCIE pulls away, lashing out.)

I'm sorry, Brucie. I'm so sorry. Please don't hate me. I'm so sorry.

(He picks the boy up, cradling him in his arms.)

I'm not what you think I am, Brucie. I'm not what you think. I'm not at all smart like you say. You're a helluva lot smarter than me, Brucie—a helluva lot smarter. See, I'm a bad boy too. I think terrible things about you. It's just that you do things that bother me, you know? Some things that you say and do really get on my nerves. I'm sorry. I am so sorry. It's all my fault.

(BRUCIE continues to sob.)

I'm gonna try Brucie. You'll see, it's gonna be better. Please forgive me.

(MICHAEL looks down.)

Brucie? Do you hate me? I love you, Brucie. I never say it, but I love you so much. Brucie? Please say that you still love me. Talk to me, baby. Talk to Mickey. Talk to me…

(MICHAEL begins to break, holding the boy closer.)

(Almost inaudibly:) It's just gonna be you and me, Brucie—just like you said. Just you and me.

(MICHAEL rocks them back and forth.)

You just go ahead and sleep, baby. Daddy will be back tomorrow. Then we'll go home, okay? You know, I bet that big black bird you saw on our walk today was a crow. That's what it was—a crow.

(Pause.)

How 'bout if I sing to you, Brucie. Would you like that? I'll sing you the song, just like you wanted…

(Softly, he sings:)

The itsy bitsy spider went up the water spout—
Down came the rain, and washed the spider out.
Out came the sun and dried up all the rain,
and the itsy bitsy spider went up the spout again…

(The lights dim slowly.)

The itsy bitsy spider went up the water spout—
Down came the rain, and washed the spider out…

(Blackout.)

HONOR AND THE RIVER

by Anton Dudley

Characters

ELIOT, 17.

HONOR, 17.

Scene

Honor is the star rower of Masterson Academy crew. Honor is also in love with Ashley Paulson who attends the girls school across the river. Forbidden by his domineering father to see Ashley, Honor has made Ashley a piece of sculpture. He needs Eliot to take it across the river for him. Eliot has been afraid of the water since his father drowned, but must now learn to swim in order to pass gym class and gain favor in the eyes of his secret crush.

Author Note

"—" is an interruption.

"..." is a short pause.

"/" is the point at which the next line of dialogue should begin, creating an overlap in speech.

> *(ELIOT and HONOR sit in a row boat on a river on the grounds of Masterson Academy Boys School. ELIOT has a blanket over his shoulders.)*

HONOR. You look like a grandma.

ELIOT. It's cold.

HONOR. You sound like a grandma.

ELIOT. Well, I'm sorry, but sitting on a river at five in the morning in late October is a very cold thing to do—regardless of one's age. I think I just saw an ice floe.

HONOR. Chill out.

ELIOT. Oh I am chilling—and if I die of hypothermia—

HONOR. What: you'll kill me?

ELIOT. Obviously not, I'll be dead.

HONOR. Fine, you can haunt me. Now stop complaining and take your sweater off. Or should I say my sweater.

ELIOT. Couldn't we do this in the pool?

HONOR. Do you have a master key to the gymnasium?

ELIOT. I think I heard someone.

HONOR. No one is here.

ELIOT. If we wait until the river freezes over, I could just skate across it and give it to her then.

HONOR. That won't happen for weeks, maybe even months.

ELIOT. Absence makes the heart / grow—

HONOR. Anyway, I thought you were Bambi?

ELIOT. I just think—

HONOR. Eliot, you made a promise!

ELIOT. All right!

HONOR. What are you so afraid of?

ELIOT. I'm not afraid.

HONOR. Why are you so afraid of admitting you're afraid?

ELIOT. I am not afraid!

HONOR. How come you never learned to swim?

ELIOT. No reason. I was just—

HONOR. Afraid?

ELIOT. Look, I know the faculty at Masterson thinks otherwise, but a good teacher does not harass his students.

HONOR. Alright. But the first thing you have to do in order to swim is get in the water... Now.

ELIOT. Don't you first want to teach me what to do once I get in there?

HONOR. I will once you're in there.

ELIOT. Won't it be a little late by then?

HONOR. Come on Eliot—

ELIOT. Although, I suppose if I do start to drown, you can just dive in and save me like you did with that "little girl" last week.

HONOR. I had to say something, my uniform was soaked.

ELIOT. And I suppose desertion was out of the question.

HONOR. My father would have killed me.

ELIOT. Instead I'm the laughing stock of the school.

HONOR. You already were anyway.

ELIOT. At least I'm not a liar.

HONOR. 'You trying to make me feel guilty? You won't.

ELIOT. Could you have at least come up with something better than "she fell from a tire swing"?

HONOR. You should have had an older brother. That's what's wrong with you. I had four: they taught me how to swim. And—everything else you don't learn in school.

ELIOT. Well, I didn't, okay? Lucky me: I just get you.

HONOR. If you freak out, don't panic; take a deep breath and hold it. If your lungs are full, you won't be able to sink, it's like having two floats right there inside you.

> *(Pause.)*

Eliot, just trust me, I'm here, nothing bad's going to happen—

ELIOT. ...You do the same, you know?

HONOR. What?

ELIOT. Talk different when you're around me.

HONOR. No I don't.

ELIOT. Yeah you do. When no one else is around, you're / more thoughtful.

HONOR. You should be careful I don't throw you in the river.

ELIOT. I thought that was the point.

HONOR. Shut up... What?

ELIOT. Nothing. I'm "shut up."

HONOR. Do you like being strange?

ELIOT. I don't mind it. I don't find many of our classmates that interesting.

HONOR. Whatever.

ELIOT. What "whatever"?

HONOR. You'd be right there in the thick of it if someone let you in.

ELIOT. Maybe. But no one has, so why sit around whining I'm not.

HONOR. Because you know you want to.

ELIOT. Obviously those friendships aren't as great as you make people think they are.

HONOR. What's that supposed to mean.

ELIOT. Who's taking your sculpture across the river?

(Pause.)

I'd like to think *my* close friends wouldn't laugh at my feelings.

HONOR. You won't be taking anything anywhere unless you take off that sweater and jump in.

ELIOT. Crud; who's that?

HONOR. No one. Everyone's asleep.

ELIOT. I heard something.

HONOR. You probably just farted.

ELIOT. No I didn't!

HONOR. I fart when I'm nervous.

ELIOT. I'm not—when are you nervous?

HONOR. I get nervous.

ELIOT. No you don't.

HONOR. Sometimes. / Sometimes I do.

ELIOT. When? I don't believe you.

HONOR. I do. Sometimes. The first time I met Ashley Paulson I farted.

ELIOT. Charming.

HONOR. She didn't hear. I controlled it. It was like stomach growling. I farted on the inside.

ELIOT. The things you do for the ones you love.

HONOR. I do love her.

ELIOT. How do you know that?

HONOR. The only person I've ever made sculpture for before was my Mom.

ELIOT. ...Do you miss her so much you don't think you're a whole person?

HONOR. Yeah, I guess. Have you ever been in love with anyone?

ELIOT. Maybe.

HONOR. Who?

ELIOT. What if I drown?

HONOR. Is that what you're afraid of?

ELIOT. It's my greatest fear in the world.

HONOR. So why are you here?

ELIOT. Oh, I don't know, it's sorta like I'm under some magic spell. Or maybe the influence of some powerful drug.

HONOR. You do drugs?

ELIOT. What? No. It was a metaphor.

HONOR. For what?

ELIOT. Never mind.

He's not the brightest bulb in the marquis, but...god his eyes are gorgeous.

HONOR. Do you hate me?

ELIOT. Why?

HONOR. 'Cause I asked you to swim.

ELIOT. No. But I do hate you.

HONOR. Why?

ELIOT. 'Cause you're the first person who's made me want to.

HONOR. ...So?

ELIOT. So.

> *(ELIOT takes off the sweater. He looks over the side of the boat.)*

So-so.

HONOR. What was that?

ELIOT. Crap. It's the grounds crew—I told you.

HONOR. We can stash the boat under the Blackberry bushes. No one ever goes near them.

ELIOT. The Blackberries?

HONOR. They grow so well 'cause they're over the septic tanks.

ELIOT. Ewh... So. Tomorrow?

HONOR. You still want to?

ELIOT. I made a promise, didn't I?

HONOR. We'll start an hour earlier.

---

13 WAYS TO SCREW UP YOUR COLLEGE INTERVIEW

by Ian McWethy

Characters

INTERVIEWER

BEN

Scene

An Interviewer must find one extra student to attend the university at which he works for or he will be fired. So far, his day has not been going well; all the potential students he's interviewed have been insane, awkward, and beyond dumb. It is at this point the Interviewer meets Ben, who seems to be a dream candidate…

(The INTERVIEWER and BEN are in mid laugh.)

BEN. And the entire audience is COMPLETELY drenched!

INTERVIEWER. Oh man! Wow!

BEN. Needless to say that was the LAST time I ever went to Sea World.

(The laughter peters out.)

INTERVIEWER. Well I've gotta tell you Ben, everything looks great. Solid SATs, GPA high above our school's average, and your essay was…well to be honest, quite moving.

BEN. Well, this is such a great university, I'd be honored to attend.

(They stand up and shake hands.)

INTERVIEWER. Hey, we'd be lucky to have you. Are you applying to any other schools?

BEN. Nope. Just here.

INTERVIEWER. Oh, okay, great. Great.

(Beat.)

BEN. So…

INTERVIEWER. Uh…yes?

BEN. I'm in then?

INTERVIEWER. Well, no. I mean not yet. I have to pass this along to my supervisors and…

> *(BEN releases his hand and sits down. Has a cold, calculating look on his face.)*

INTERVIEWER. It's a process, you know, I can't officially—

BEN. *(Dead pan and intense:)* Sit down.

INTERVIEWER. What?

BEN. Sit down, won't you?

> *(The INTERVIEWER sits down.)*

INTERVIEWER. Is there a problem?

BEN. That depends on you. You see, for reasons I can't entirely explain to you at this moment, it is vital that I attend this University. I've been meticulously planning for this day, years of SAT prep, AP classes, all in the hopes of being accepted. I was intending to hear an answer today.

INTERVIEWER. Well, I'm sorry, I…don't have the authority to just let you in right now.

BEN. There are forces at play here friend, forces that you cannot possibly comprehend. But trust me, it is very vital, and not just for me, but for the entire student body and faculty that I am enrolled for the fall semester. Many lives hang in the balance. You don't want to be held responsible for the loss of life, do you?

INTERVIEWER. Of course not…but…how is me letting you in today going to save lives?

BEN. The world is a series of connections and plans, every human being affects another, every decision has a consequence, and this decision…this decision will be the most important one you'll ever make.

INTERVIEWER. Ben, you're being incredibly vague and…besides, it's not as simple as "me letting you in."

BEN. An oral agreement is legally binding in this state. So, in fact, it is that simple.

INTERVIEWER. Look, what I can tell you is that it's practically a done deal, I'm going to give you a great recommendation, and with your stats—

BEN. THAT'S NOT…what I'm asking for.

> *(Tense beat.)*

INTERVIEWER. Ben, let's not ruin what was a great interview by—

BEN. I'm not leaving until I get my answer.

INTERVIEWER. Well you're going to have to because I have another prospective coming in at one.

BEN. No you don't. Your four o'clock cancelled this morning. You don't have another appointment until Rebecca Smith at 4:45.

(Beat. The INTERVIEWER is now kinda freaked out.)

INTERVIEWER. How did you...did you break into my e-mail or something?

(BEN looks straight ahead.)

INTERVIEWER. Okay, you know what, I'm not sure what happened here, but I'm going to have to call security.

(The INTERVIEWER picks up the phone. He clicks the receiver a couple of times.)

INTERVIEWER. Hello I...hello, hello?

BEN. Phone troubles?

(The INTERVIEWER slowly puts the phone down. He gets up and backs away.)

BEN. Doors locked. And we're ten stories up so the windows wouldn't be a very...safe option either.

INTERVIEWER. Alright, who are you?

BEN. A name is but a label, and I have many labels but that's not important right now. What's important is that you, tell me, right now...exactly what I was hoping to hear.

INTERVIEWER. Ben if I could I would, it's just—

(The lights go out. BEN immediately turns on a flashlight, underlighting his face. When the INTERVIEWER talks, he points the light on him.)

BEN. It's only an outage friend. Circuits break all the time.

INTERVIEWER. Please, I don't have any real authority. An acceptance from me would be meaningless—

BEN. Then there's no reason not to say it.

INTERVIEWER. Why are you doing this?

BEN. I'm not doing this, you're doing this. And it can all go away with three little words—

INTERVIEWER. But it won't—

BEN. NO! THOSE AREN'T THE RIGHT WORDS! SAY IT! JUST SAY IT!

INTERVIEWER. Okay! I…you've been accepted. You've been accepted. You'll be enrolled in the fall semester upon hearing of your acceptance.

> *(The lights come back on. BEN turns the lights off. A tense moment, then…)*

BEN. *(Switching back:)* Oh man! That's great! I can't even tell you how… I gotta call my mom. It was so nice to meet you.

> *(BEN cheerily leaves the room. The INTERVIEWER collapses into his seat.)*

CONSPICUOUS

by Winter Miller

Characters

JOSEPH, a new father.

ANTHONY, his friend.

Scene

Anthony and Joseph are wandering in search of a daycare center, or so Joseph would have him believe.

> *(ANTHONY and JOSEPH walk a fairly deserted street in a residential neighborhood. ANTHONY carries a large radio. JOSEPH carries an open knapsack with a baby in it.)*

ANTHONY. But see either way I make a profit because I got it for almost nothing and if I want to, I can use it for a few months and then sell it. It's just I have to get the junk that's in the battery area out, but otherwise it's in perfect condition, got one tiny scratch on the bottom that you wouldn't even see. I'm going to always ask for the store model, man, that's how you get this stuff for cheap. I get this green stuff out with like a knife or something and it looks new. I know it works, I made sure of that. I could probably make at least 40 bucks on it. Or maybe I could go around to electronic stores and buy the store models and then I could sell them on the street or wherever for a 300% markup, that's what I should do, make me a little money. Although I was thinking I could give it to my moms because she filled out all those forms for me and this could be kind of like a thank you, plus I would still get to use it. She would be impressed if I did that. Maybe I will do that and I can go back and get the next store model in a couple of months and start my resale business. But you know what she said—

JOSEPH. Anthony.

ANTHONY. What?

JOSEPH. Do you listen to yourself?

ANTHONY. No. I hear it when I say it I don't have to then sit there and listen to it again.

JOSEPH. Man, shut up. You're just jabbering.

ANTHONY. I was talking, I was telling you my business idea.

JOSEPH. You're talking about batteries and—

73

ANTHONY. Forget it man. I was thinking I would cut you in. But forget it.

JOSEPH. Can we just have silence.

ANTHONY. Where is this place?

JOSEPH. Down a little further.

ANTHONY. What's the number?

JOSEPH. The number?

ANTHONY. Of the place where we're going. What's with you man?

JOSEPH. It's just down there more.

ANTHONY. Are we lost?

JOSEPH. No. I said it's down there.

ANTHONY. But what's the number then?

JOSEPH. 690. Shut up.

ANTHONY. Where's Shawna at?

JOSEPH. What?

ANTHONY. Shawna?

JOSEPH. She's at work.

ANTHONY. You didn't tell me she got a job.

JOSEPH. She works at Wendy's.

ANTHONY. How long she been there?

JOSEPH. Two days.

ANTHONY. They still hiring?

JOSEPH. I don't know. Go ask.

ANTHONY. I like those hamburgers. Square. Frosties are good too. She get free food there?

JOSEPH. No.

ANTHONY. She come home with stuff though at the end of the night? Like the burgers and fries that didn't get eaten?

JOSEPH. *(Exasperated:)* I don't know.

ANTHONY. Okay. Never mind then. What's wrong with you?

JOSEPH. Nothing.

ANTHONY. I'm hungry.

> *(They walk in silence.)*

ANTHONY. If you saw this in a store, how much you pay for it?

JOSEPH. I wouldn't.

ANTHONY. You in a pissed off mood. Where is this place? You said it wasn't that far. I'm carrying this around for like blocks… This is 304 and that's the end of the street so I don't know where you think the 600s are gonna be. This is a pain in the ass place for a daycare center to be anyway, who comes all the way out here for this?

JOSEPH. These people here use it.

ANTHONY. But why are you using it? Why can't your mom watch her?

JOSEPH. She's busy.

ANTHONY. How much does day care cost every hour?

JOSEPH. I don't know.

ANTHONY. They didn't say nothing over the phone, like it's ten dollars for the whole day or something?

JOSEPH. No.

ANTHONY. Is it one of those places where it's just like in somebody's house?

JOSEPH. Yeah.

ANTHONY. I saw this thing on the news about places that aren't licensed and the teachers were molesting all the kids. Sick, man. The boys and the girls. You better check this place out good if you don't know about it.

JOSEPH. Why you runnin' your mouth man? It's none of your business.

ANTHONY. That's just a park through there, the numbers stop here. You have a cross street for this place?

(JOSEPH sets the baby down on the sidewalk in the knapsack. He turns and walks back the way he came.)

ANTHONY. I have to get back and help my brother move his furniture. What are you doing?

(JOSEPH keeps walking.)

ANTHONY. Hey!

(ANTHONY looks down at the baby. He hurries off in the direction of JOSEPH.)

LUNCH

by Shawn Northrip

Characters

DMITRY

BEN

Scene

Best friends since fourth grade, this is the last time Ben and Dmitry ever speak to each other.

> *(BEN sits at table writing. At his feet is a guitar case. On the table, next to his notepad, is a sack lunch.)*
>
> *(DMITRY approaches with a school lunch. He puts down the tray.)*

DMITRY. What'cha working on?

BEN. *(Nothing:)* You know.

DMITRY. Seriously, Benny, show me. You don't keep secrets from me.

> *(DMITRY flicks BEN in the ear.)*

BEN. Ow. Man.

> *(BEN slides the paper across the table. DMITRY reads it over.)*

DMITRY. Is this about me?

BEN. Not everything is about you.

DMITRY. This is.

BEN. Come on.

> *(BEN grabs it back.)*

DMITRY. That's us at the beach last year when we met that girl. What was her name? Sandy? Summer?

BEN. Jocelyn. And no, it's not.

> *(DMITRY grabs the paper back.)*

DMITRY. Yes it is. I remember, see here, I made you do all the embarrassing work like meeting her, and convincing her to hang out, and then I got to make out with her.

BEN. It's a piece of fiction. Why do you have to read into everything?

76

DMITRY. Why do you have to write about everything?

BEN. I don't. It's just a stupid story.

DMITRY. Either way, no homework at the lunch table.

    (BEN grabs it back.)

BEN. It's not homework.

DMITRY. Just put it away.

BEN. Okay. *(He does.)* The weather is nice today, maybe after school we could go throw some rocks at traffic.

DMITRY. I can't. I'm going over to Vanessa's house.

BEN. Again? We went over there yesterday.

DMITRY. Ben, it's just me this time.

BEN. Oh.

DMITRY. Yeah.

BEN. So, it's finally the big day.

DMITRY. Well, no. Vanessa doesn't really like you.

BEN. She doesn't like me? What's not to like about me?

DMITRY. That's what I said to her. I said, "Ben's the funniest guy I know. No one can duck his head and run into a locker like him."

BEN. I dented the crap out of like ten lockers.

DMITRY. You see, I think that's awesome.

BEN. At her party the other week, I kept sticking my head in her toilet to entertain her guests.

DMITRY. She thinks you're childish.

BEN. I'm childish?

DMITRY. And her little sister said you were a bad kisser.

BEN. Her little sister is like eleven. What does she know about kissing?

DMITRY. You were the one making out with her.

BEN. You made me.

DMITRY. But I didn't make you suck.

BEN. She's the bad kisser.

DMITRY. I thought she was a good kisser.

BEN. You kissed your girlfriend's sister?

DMITRY. Vanessa said I could.

BEN. Why?

DMITRY. How else was I supposed to know if you are a bad kisser or not unless I knew Shelly could kiss?

BEN. You conned your girlfriend into letting you make out with her eleven-year-old sister?

DMITRY. She called you a dish washer. She said you scrubbed her teeth clean with your tongue.

BEN. I did not. I am not a bad kisser.

DMITRY. Well, there's only one way to prove it to me.

BEN. You're kidding me.

DMITRY. You're gonna have to do it.

BEN. I am not going to French you.

DMITRY. Before this argument goes any further, let's recap our friendship. In the five years we've been best friends how many times have I suggested something stupid for you to do that you didn't want?

BEN. More than I care to count.

DMITRY. And how many of those things did you end up doing?

BEN. All of them.

DMITRY. So why continue to argue?

BEN. Because it's what I do best.

DMITRY. Maybe it'd help if I put you in the mood? Maybe if I massage your shoulders a bit?

BEN. Give it up.

DMITRY. What do you want to do this weekend?

BEN. Don't you have to be on Vanessa's leash?

DMITRY. She's at her grandmother's, so lucky for you, I'm free all weekend. Until she gets back on Sunday.

BEN. Saturday night I'm spending the night over at Jeff's.

DMITRY. That's the third week in a row.

BEN. Well, I'm sorry about that but remember I'm never invited to the make out parties at Vanessa's house. While you've been over there getting TMJ, I had to find something else to do with my weekends.

DMITRY. Is he your new best friend?

BEN. No. I already have a best friend.

DMITRY. Because, you know you can be honest with me. If you don't want to be my friend anymore, just tell me. Cut me loose. Don't lead me on.

BEN. I'm not "breaking up" with you.

DMITRY. Then cancel on Jeff.

BEN. I can't.

DMITRY. You know he's just gonna hurt you.

BEN. Don't be jealous.

DMITRY. What are you gonna do with him that you can't do with me?

BEN. What do you do with Vanessa that you can't do with me? …Don't answer that.

DMITRY. Fine. Go make out with your boyfriend.

BEN. We're just gonna listen to his dad's old Jimi Hendrix records.

DMITRY. You better remember that I was the one who introduced you to Jimi Hendrix, and Guns and Roses, and the Misfits. Before me, you just listened to showtunes.

BEN. You made me the person I am. Fine. And I made you…well…I guess you find me entertaining. Somehow.

DMITRY. You're loyal. I respect that.

BEN. Well, how about Friday?

DMITRY. I'm going to the dance with Vanessa.

BEN. Oh. Right.

DMITRY. Thursday?

BEN. Guitar lessons. Wednesday?

DMITRY. Sports banquet. I'm getting two M.V.P.'s. And the scholarship to basketball camp this summer.

BEN. How about a week from Saturday?

DMITRY. Make out party. *(Suddenly has an idea.)* Oh, this is it, man. This is the brainstorm. This is the idea to end all ideas. I can get you invited to the make out parties, if, get this, if we get you a girlfriend.

BEN. Who?

DMITRY. Franchine.

BEN. Aw, Franchine.

DMITRY. It's perfect.

BEN. Why not ask me to date Brynn while you're at it?

DMITRY. Cause Brynn won't get you invited to the party.

BEN. Why can't I have a cool girl?

DMITRY. *(Yeah, right:)* Ben.

BEN. You could have at least offered me Britney.

DMITRY. Oh, come on.

BEN. But Britney's the ugliest of the group. She's the sympathy friend.

DMITRY. Vanessa's very protective about Britney. They have a long history together. Or they have history together, one of the two.

BEN. So she won't trust me with her pet?

DMITRY. Maybe if you got some nicer clothes.

BEN. What's wrong with my clothes? You never complained about my clothes before.

DMITRY. I'm just trying to help you out.

BEN. I don't need that kind of help.

DMITRY. I don't like this new negative side of yours.

BEN. Here's my plan instead, why don't you ditch Vanessa and we can go ride bikes.

DMITRY. I'm selling my bike.

BEN. You'd really rather sell your bike than break up with a girl? You love that bike. You searched for three months to find the perfect pegs with the hearts on the ends. And you just got it chrome-dipped.

DMITRY. I'm not breaking up with Vanessa. And I need the money.

BEN. What do you need money for? Her family is loaded. She buys you everything you want.

DMITRY. Her family is taking me to the beach this summer and I'd like to do something nice for them.

BEN. I thought we always go to the beach together.

DMITRY. I'll go with you too.

BEN. What's the point of going to the beach with a girl? She's not gonna check out the other girls with you. And you'll have to spend all your time with her.

DMITRY. So.

BEN. She's not going to want to go swimming at night. She won't be willing to try to catch jelly fish, or pretend to be your foreign language translator, or ride the Vominator.

DMITRY. You never rode the Vominator.

BEN. No, but I laughed when you puked. You think she'll laugh when you puke?

DMITRY. I'm acting like I'm going into the ninth grade, you're acting like you're going into sixth.

(Silence.)

(BEN takes out his notepad and starts to write again. DMITRY real-izes he wounded his friend.)

Remember that time we were lying in the road and that lady in the minivan pulled up and said, "You want to die?" And you were like, "Hey, soccer mom, guess what? Soccer sucks!" That was pretty awesome. You got a way with words, "Soccer sucks." Genius.

(BEN does not look up.)

You remember that time when we crushed those SweetTarts into a powder and then snorted it until we got high. That was pretty dumb, huh?

(BEN is ignoring DMITRY.)

Remember that time I told you I ran away to West Virginia and you packed your stuff to come find me, but when you came out your front door, I was sitting in your yard.

(BEN stops writing, but does not look up.)

You ever get the feeling like it's one of those moments that you know you'll remember forever?

(BEN looks up and nods.)

So, you want to hug before I take off, just in case.

(They hug, it is brief, very guy-hug. DMITRY takes his lunch and exits.)

Scenes for One Man and One Woman

DOG ACT

by Liz Duffy Adams

Characters

DOG, a young male. Human by birth, dog by choice. His dog behavior is minimal and subtle. When he barks, as indicated, he does not make barking sounds; he shouts the word "bark."

VERA, gray-haired woman.

Scene

In a post-apocalyptic future, Dog and Vera have re-met by chance in the ruins of the "university tribe" they both came from. He is a young man who lives humbly as a dog in repentance for his past, which he is now terrified Vera will reveal. She is older, a sooth-sayer and survivor, determined to force Dog to take her side in an approaching fight.

VERA. Strange, isn't it? It must be perfectly surreal, not to say nightmarish, for you, finding yourself here again, after so long. It's strange enough for me. Quite numbingly painful, even for me, at first.

DOG. I don't. I don't know what. What you.

VERA. It's possible, I grant, that you don't remember me. You were young. Still of an age to find most adults interchangeable. I slept on the far side of the, what did we call it? The campus. I think it was over there, my tower. Though it's curiously difficult to get my bearings. It's so much altered. The place where we both were born. Where I grew up, worked, made plans. Till the sky fell and everything ended.

DOG. I've never. Been here. Never seen. You. Or this. Place.

VERA. Do you not remember who I am? Now, I mean to say, who I am now. I cannot lie. I tell only the truth. Not the whole truth, but nothing but the truth. You may not remember me. But I know you. I know what you did, boy.

(Slight pause.)

DOG. Are you going to kill me?

VERA. Is that what you want?

DOG. It doesn't matter.

VERA. Are you inviting me to pity you?

DOG. No.

VERA. How did it happen, precisely? I've so often wondered.

Am I not entitled to know?

DOG. I wanted to know. What was outside the walls. Everyone said terrible things. But I knew that grown-ups didn't always tell the truth. I didn't believe them. I wanted to know. So I slipped away. I went to the South Gate. I knew the watchman that time and day was my uncle Fig. I knew he got sleepy after lunch. I waited till he dozed off and I opened the gate. I only meant to look. But there was that little ridge, that I couldn't see over. I found I had to just see what was on the other side. And there were woods, and there was something through the trees, and I found I just had to go see what that was. It was a stream, running off down a slope, and I followed it. After I'd walked for a while I got tired, and I lay among some ferns to rest. And I fell asleep. When I woke up it was nearly dark. I was worried. I'd have been missed by then. How would I explain? I followed the stream back, and went through the little woods, and climbed up the ridge. I began to hear a noise. I came to the top of the ridge.

VERA. You'd left the gate open.

DOG. I'd left the gate open.

How did you survive?

VERA. Some of the women they didn't kill.

I often, later, wondered what became of you.

DOG. I became a dog.

My mother. Was she.

VERA. She fought too valiantly to be captured. An arrow pierced her brain, through an eye.

DOG. Didn't you fight too?

VERA. Oh, no. I surrendered instantly. By the end of the first day's captivity I was the slave of the head-man. At the end of a week, he was mine. I wasn't beautiful, mind you.

DOG. I know what you were.

VERA. Are you judging me?

DOG. No.

VERA. Surely it isn't necessary to remind you.

DOG. No.

VERA. It is strange, being here again. If I didn't know better, I would say there's a feeling here of unquiet ghosts. Do you feel that? Restless spirits of the betrayed and unavenged.

DOG. They. They wouldn't have wanted.

VERA. Wouldn't have wanted revenge? They were a gentle people. But they were most ungently served. No doubt you imagine that your own suffering, your voluntary demotion from humanity, your assumption of canine humility are sufficient to shield you from your own past deeds. It doesn't work that way, dear boy, as you ought to know. It is a matter of consequences. Not a moral question at all. There are things that forgiveness cannot touch. There are things that once done cannot be undone. Do you understand me? Feeling any amount of guilt or anguish, performing any little rites of expiation, all that is quite beside the point, because it isn't a sin, a personal moral drama—it is an historical fact. A miniature civilization lies here in ruins and decay. Because of you. I stand here as the sole survivor of your act of thoughtlessness and selfishness. The sole surviving member of your own tribe. Your only kin in this world, and your victim. Can you look at me and deny me anything? Can you look at me and not know that you belong to me, body and, for what it's worth, soul?

DOG. No.

VERA. That's right.

I'm glad we've had this chance to talk. I'm sure it's a relief to you, in a way. You've come home. All you need do now is remember where your allegiance lies. I won't ask anything else from you. Do you understand me, Dog?

DOG. Yes.

TO KNOW KNOW KNOW ME

by Courtney Baron

Characters

PHILLIP

EMILY

Scene

Emily, an insecure girl desperate to be noticed, has just told her boyfriend, Phillip, that she is going to be on *American Idol*.

Author Note

When dialogue appears in brackets, feel free to update the cultural reference.

PHILLIP. Shut up. Shut up. Shut up.

EMILY. No it's true.

PHILLIP. That's sick.

EMILY. I know.

PHILLIP. Sick!

EMILY. I know.

PHILLIP. Does your mom know?

EMILY. No.

PHILLIP. You should call her.

EMILY. She'll be pissed.

PHILLIP. You think she'll be pissed?

EMILY. Yes.

PHILLIP. Naw.

EMILY. She will.

PHILLIP. She's going to be proud.

EMILY. I skipped school.

PHILLIP. Good cause, you know, good cause.

EMILY. I don't know.

PHILLIP. I'm telling you—

EMILY. I know.

PHILLIP. I'm just saying—

EMILY. I know.

PHILLIP. Do you love me?

EMILY. I do.

PHILLIP. Then trust me.

EMILY. I do.

PHILLIP. Call your mom.

EMILY. I'll tell her later.

PHILLIP. This is big.

EMILY. I know.

PHILLIP. You're going to be on *American Idol*.

EMILY. I know.

PHILLIP. Wait.

EMILY. What?

PHILLIP. You going to get big and love me less?

EMILY. No.

PHILLIP. Come on, you'll be driving 'round in limos, doing your thing and I'll be back here and you won't even know me.

EMILY. I'll always know you.

PHILLIP. And you'll be known.

EMILY. I guess so.

PHILLIP. Sick.

EMILY. I know.

PHILLIP. I didn't even know you'd signed up.

EMILY. Yeah. I guess. I forgot to tell you.

PHILLIP. What'd you sing?

EMILY. Phillip, I'm hungry.

PHILLIP. You want to go out?

EMILY. No.

PHILLIP. What do you want?

EMILY. Nevermind. I'm not. I'm not really hungry.

PHILLIP. Alright.

EMILY. I'm going home.

PHILLIP. What?

EMILY. I'm tired.

PHILLIP. How the hell can you be tired?

EMILY. I lied.

PHILLIP. What?

EMILY. I lied.

PHILLIP. What does that mean?

EMILY. I was at the library.

PHILLIP. What?

EMILY. All day today. I took the 2 train to the big library in Brooklyn.

PHILLIP. Are you kidding me?

EMILY. No.

PHILLIP. What?

EMILY. I'm going home.

PHILLIP. I don't think so.

EMILY. You don't get to choose.

PHILLIP. You lied.

EMILY. I lied.

PHILLIP. You're a liar.

EMILY. I guess so.

PHILLIP. Hell.

EMILY. I hate you.

PHILLIP. What?

EMILY. Nevermind. I didn't mean that.

PHILLIP. What the hell is wrong with you?

EMILY. Nothing. Don't judge me.

PHILLIP. Are you serious?

EMILY. You always judge me.

PHILLIP. I don't.

EMILY. Do more. Be more.

PHILLIP. Sure, I want you to do things.

EMILY. Maybe I can't.

PHILLIP. You can.

EMILY. I don't think so. You want me to be someone I'm not.

PHILLIP. You lied to me.

EMILY. I'm leaving.

PHILLIP. Go ahead.

EMILY. I am.

PHILLIP. Go ahead.

EMILY. Really.

PHILLIP. Really. Go. Ahead.

(*She doesn't leave.*)

EMILY. But you want me to go, right? Because I'm a liar?

PHILLIP. You're like a crazy person.

EMILY. I think you're right, I'm crazy.

PHILLIP. So get some help.

EMILY. I want you to help me.

PHILLIP. Emily.

EMILY. I just want you to think I'm special.

PHILLIP. I do.

EMILY. No you don't.

PHILLIP. Don't tell me how I feel.

EMILY. When you look at me, I see how boring I am.

PHILLIP. You're tiring.

EMILY. And then when we're watching TV, your face lights up, you see [Mariah Carey] singing or [Beyoncé] doing some commercial and it's like something in you just gets smiley. I want to do that.

PHILLIP. Emily that's stupid.

EMILY. I know.

PHILLIP. You think I'm like [Jay-Z]? Or who's that one you like from that movie about the car? Am I like that?

EMILY. I don't need you to be.

PHILLIP. But I need you to be a movie star? I don't think so.

EMILY. I want to be somebody else.

PHILLIP. Go ahead. But don't come at me with crazy lies.

EMILY. You love me?

PHILLIP. When you're honest.

EMILY. So for the few minutes I was lying you didn't love me.

PHILLIP. No.

EMILY. Just like that?

PHILLIP. Don't try to mix this up.

EMILY. I want you to do something for me. I want you to just for one day, I want you to pretend like I did make it on *American Idol* and that maybe I'd be somebody.

PHILLIP. That's crazy.

EMILY. I'm a little crazy.

PHILLIP. You need to get some medicine for your crazy.

EMILY. Okay, but maybe just for today, if you want to help me a little bit. Come on Phillip. Come on…
You were excited, admit it.

PHILLIP. So.

EMILY. So, let's get you excited again.

PHILLIP. Are you coming on to me?

EMILY. Not everything is about doing it.

PHILLIP. Emily.

EMILY. If I could just change one thing, do one thing—

PHILLIP. What does that mean?

EMILY. If I could be somebody.

(Silence.)

PHILLIP. Okay.

EMILY. Okay?

PHILLIP. What do you want me to do?

EMILY. Treat me like I'm known.

PHILLIP. I don't know how to do that.

EMILY. Try.

PHILLIP. "Hey, do I know you?"

EMILY. "I don't think so."

PHILLIP. "I do."

EMILY. "You do?"

(The game ends.)

PHILLIP. Yes.

EMILY. You know me?

PHILLIP. Isn't it enough if I know you?

(Pause, she thinks about it.)

EMILY. No. I don't think it's enough. I don't think it is.

PHILLIP. Should I believe you? I mean you're a liar, right?

EMILY. Come on, I'm Emily, you *know* me.

PHILLIP. I want to be real here. Be honest.

EMILY. Don't be.

PHILLIP. I have to. Emily, I don't know you.

EMILY. Nobody does. Not even me. But if I had gotten on *American Idol*…

PHILLIP. What?

EMILY. Maybe they'd make me into somebody you'd try harder to know.

FIREBIRDS

by Liz Flahive

Characters

ADAM, a senior in high school.

MELANIE, his sister, a sophmore.

Scene

Adam and Melanie's parents have recently decided to get a divorce and it's making the end of the school year even harder on both of them. It's a week before graduation.

(ADAM and MELANIE sit on a bench outside the principal's office.)

ADAM. Would you rather be a midget or a giant?

MELANIE. Midget. Definitely. Would you rather have one tiny malformed arm or one gimpy leg?

ADAM. Arm.

MELANIE. Really?

ADAM. Little Arm.

MELANIE. Oookay. Wow. Little arm.

ADAM. Would you rather have a purple face and a green body or a green face and a purple body?

MELANIE. That's the same thing.

ADAM. It's not at all.

MELANIE. Adam. It's the same thing. Either way you've got a purple something and a green something else.

ADAM. Would you rather...

MELANIE. Fine. Purple face.

ADAM. Interesting.

MELANIE. No it's not. It's not a choice and that question tells you nothing about me.

ADAM. Oh. I disagree.

MELANIE. Whatever. Would you rather live in Dad's apartment or Mom's house?

ADAM. Pass.

MELANIE. No. No passing.

ADAM. Pass.

MELANIE. Fine. Then I win.

ADAM. That's not a good question. I mean, it's a good question but it's not fun.

MELANIE. But it tells me something about you. Doesn't it.

ADAM. Would you rather sit in between Mom and Dad and referee at graduation or wait here with me for another 30 minutes to get them seats on opposite sides of the auditorium.

MELANIE. Wait here with you. That's easy. *(Beat.)* So when were you going to tell me you're not going to Iowa State.

ADAM. It's not a big deal.

MELANIE. Yeah. Totally not a big deal to get into college and then not go.

ADAM. I can't make Mom and Dad pay thousands of dollars for something I don't really care about.

MELANIE. Is this because they're getting divorced?

ADAM. No.

MELANIE. Is this because of that girl?

ADAM. No.

MELANIE. Because I think it's about that girl.

ADAM. She has a name, Melanie.

MELANIE. Just because you've had sex doesn't mean you know everything and now you don't have to go to college.

> *(He punches her in the arm. She punches him back.)*

MELANIE. I don't get it. They wait until you graduate to split up. But I have to deal with joint custody for two years.

ADAM. Yeah. They love me more.

MELANIE. Have you like, thought this through? At all?

ADAM. Look dude. Let's just get them seats for graduation that won't be right next to each other.

> *(Pause.)*

ADAM. Would you rather spend the rest of your life trapped in an elevator with Josh Oshinsky or eat a handful of live bees.

MELANIE. Live bees.

ADAM. You're allergic. You'll probably die.

MELANIE. Live bees.

ADAM. Wow. You love him. You want to get drunk and make out with him again.

MELANIE. Okay shut up I never should have told you that ever.

> *(Looking around the office:)*

I can't believe I have two more years in this hellhole.

> *(They wait. Bell rings as the lights fade.)*

LITTLE WOMEN

adapted by Jacqueline Goldfinger
from the novel by Louisa May Alcott

Chararacters

JO, 17-18, tomboy, wants to have an adventure.

LAURIE, 19-20, Jo's best friend, exuberant, not very proper.

Scene

Laurie has fallen in love with his neighbor, Josephine. While Jo and Laurie are great friends, she has ignored his romantic overtures. When Laurie asks Jo to marry him she rejects him while still trying to maintain their friendship. Set in an upper class neighborhood in 1860s Concord, Massachusetts.

LAURIE. I finish school next week.

JO. "Hail the conquering hero comes!" Beth is making you a cake. Oh, but don't tell her that I told you, it's a surprise.

LAURIE. I will look very surprised.

    (LAURIE makes a "surprised" face.)

JO. Perfect!

LAURIE. Grandfather thinks I should travel for the summer before returning to work. He says it's good for a young man to know the world.

JO. But you've already traveled.

LAURIE. I think, I think he wants me to see my old friends one last time, before settling down into...work...marriage.

    (LAURIE looks at her slyly. JO doesn't notice.)

JO. We will miss you horribly.

LAURIE. Will you—

JO. *(Melodramatic:)* Yes, it will be like Rodrigo's men stabbed me in the heart and drew it out of my body still beating!

LAURIE. No, Jo, I meant, will you—

JO. Of course, I will. You will have to tell me all about it. And postcards, I want lots of postcards with beautiful pictures of places I should visit someday.

LAURIE. I don't want to go alone.

(A long beat.)

JO. But you'll see all of your old friends.

LAURIE. Yes, and I'd like to introduce them to someone.

(Takes a deep breath.)

I'd like to introduce them…to my wife.

(A beat.)

So will you please—

(JO places her hands over his mouth to muffle him.)

JO. Oh, no, Laurie, don't.

(JO removes her hands.)

LAURIE. *(Rushed:)* I've loved you ever since I've known you, Jo, couldn't help it, you've been so good to me, for me. I've tried to show it.

JO. I thought you understood.

LAURIE. Girls, they're so queer, you never know what they mean. They say "no" when they mean "yes" and drive a man out of his wits just for the fun of it.

JO. I don't.

LAURIE. I know. And so I loved you all the more, though I'm not half good enough…

JO. You, you are, you're a great deal too good for me, and I'm so grateful to you, and so proud and fond of you, I don't see why I can't love you as you want me to. I've thought about it and I've tried, but I can't change the feeling of friendship into love. It would be a lie to say I do when I don't. I could never lie to you, Laurie.

LAURIE. But have you really thought about it and truly tried?

JO. I have.

(A long beat.)

Oh, Laurie, I'm sorry.

(A long beat.)

I can't help it. It's impossible for people to make themselves love other people if they don't.

LAURIE. They do sometimes.

JO. I don't believe that's the right sort of love, and I'd rather not try it.

LAURIE. I can't love anyone else.

JO. You will. You will fall madly in love with a wonderful and accomplished girl, and I will be there to celebrate your wedding, as a friend.

LAURIE. Please, just, think about it.

JO. We are not suited to each other, my quick temper and our strong wills would make us miserable.

LAURIE. If you would only marry me, Jo, I would be a perfect saint.

JO. I am your friend for who you are, I don't wish for you to be otherwise.

(*A long beat.*)

LAURIE. I don't believe you've got any heart.

JO. I wish I hadn't. I wouldn't feel so awful right now.

(*LAURIE stands, straightens himself, collects the shards of his heart, but can't look her in the eye.*)

JO. You will find a fine mistress for your beautiful mansion. I'm homely and awkward and never liked elegant society, but you do, and someday you'd hate me, and my scribbling, and I couldn't get on without it, and we should be unhappy, and wish we hadn't done it.

(*JO takes his face in her hands, forces him to look at her.*)

JO. The night of the Moffat's Ball, you stayed, you didn't come home to read with me. I knew then that you were still looking for your home. And it's not me.

(*A beat.*)

LAURIE. Anything more?

JO. Nothing, except that I don't believe I shall ever marry. I'm happy as I am.

LAURIE. You may think so now, but there will come a time when you will love someone, tremendously, live and die for him, and I shall have to stand by and see it. And that will ruin me.

(*LAURIE exits.*

JO's alone.)

A DOLL'S HOUSE IS A METAPHOR

by Patrick Greene

Characters

NORA, a high school age girl. Not very bright.

KROGSTAD, he likes to pretend he's a movie villain, but he's a nerd to the core.

Scene

Krogstad, an odd young fellow, has just been fired from his job by Nora's boyfriend. In order to get his job back, he's blackmailing Nora, but it's not going to be easy because Nora is, well, a bit dim.

(The front door swings open and in the doorways stands KROGSTAD, a bespectacled and acne-riddled teenager.)

NORA. Krogstad, what are you doing here?

KROGSTAD. Nora, it is I, Krogstad!

NORA. I know, I just said that.

KROGSTAD. You are probably wondering what I'm doing here.

NORA. I just said...

KROGSTAD. I will tell you why I am here.

(An awkward pause.)

NORA. Why are you here?

KROGSTAD. I am here to threaten you.

NORA. *(Shocked:)* You mustn't.

KROGSTAD. Oh yes... I must.

NORA. But life is perfect.

KROGSTAD. You see, little Nora, your beloved Torvald has fired me and hired that fox, Christine. As you may know, my popularity level at school had dropped significantly since the unfortunate public pantsing incident last year, and my position at Frankie's was my first step in reclaiming my popularity. Now that your boyfriend has fired me, I am a ruined man.

NORA. I don't understand. What does all this have to do with me?

KROGSTAD. Do I really have to spell it out for you?

NORA. Yes.

KROGSTAD. I'm the one who put your forged ballots through in the school council election.

NORA. Uh huh.

KROGSTAD. Your boyfriend is a manager at Frankie's Diner.

NORA. I see.

KROGSTAD. You really haven't figured it out?

NORA. No.

KROGSTAD. I'm going to speak very slowly, so you can understand me. If you don't make Torvald give me my job back then I'm going to tell everyone that you forged the ballots and Torvald will be impeached.

NORA. I don't get it.

KROGSTAD. I'm threatening you!

NORA. *(Shocked:)* No, you mustn't.

KROGSTAD. I already have.

NORA. But what am I to do?

KROGSTAD. You must get me my job back.

NORA. But Torvald despises you. He says you smell like cheese.

KROGSTAD. Nevertheless, if I do not have my job back by tomorrow evening, I will tell everyone that you forged the ballots, starting with Torvald, who will promptly dump you.

NORA. No, you mustn't.

KROGSTAD. I shall.

(*An awkward pause.*)

NORA. Aren't you going to leave now?

KROGSTAD. I…I have to go to the bathroom.

NORA. It's through the hall. Second door on the left.

(*KROGSTAD goes to the hall. Stops.*)

KROGSTAD. I shall leave the toilet seat up.

NORA. *(Shocked as before:)* No, you mustn't.

KROGSTAD. You can't stop me.

(*KROGSTAD exits off into the hallway. After a brief moment he returns. This time he has the posture and voice of an awkward teenager.*)

KROGSTAD. I was pretty frightening, wasn't I?

NORA. Yes, you were simply devastating.

KROGSTAD. I've been practicing with my little sister for the past two hours. I made her cry a couple of times, but she's only three.

NORA. Still, you were very believable.

KROGSTAD. Thank you. I have to go to the bathroom now. I'm sorry about the toilet seat thing. I got a little carried away. I'll put it down.

NORA. Thank you.

> *(KROGSTAD exits through the hallway.)*

(Note: *A Doll's House is a Metaphor* is part of the full-length play *Ibsen Undone*.)

FREAK

by Naomi Iizuka and Ryan Pavelchik

Characters

STRAIGHT A GIRL

SUPER ACHIEVER

Scene

Sraight A Girl sees admission to Harvard as the golden ticket to a successful future, but Super Achiever Boy is preoccupied by a morally ambigous act he may or may not have already committed.

> *(An empty classroom. STRAIGHT A GIRL and SUPER ACHIEVER BOY work on their college applications together.)*

STRAIGHT A GIRL. Do you think we'll get in?

SUPER ACHIEVER BOY. I don't know.

STRAIGHT A GIRL. I sense doubt. Doubt will kill you.

SUPER ACHIEVER BOY. Harvard is a long shot. Even with a 4.0, stellar recs, and a million extracurriculars, it's still a long shot. We're competing against Olympic athletes and child celebrities and people who were like home-schooled in like…Utah. You know. Interesting people.

STRAIGHT A GIRL. We're fascinating.

SUPER ACHIEVER BOY. Not really.

STRAIGHT A GIRL. All we need is like a special skill.

SUPER ACHIEVER BOY. I know that. You think I don't know that?

STRAIGHT A GIRL. In my spare time, I'm an amateur archeologist. My favorite city is Pompeii.

SUPER ACHIEVER BOY. No.

STRAIGHT A GIRL. Pastry chef. I like to bake cakes and pies and cinnamon buns.

SUPER ACHIEVER BOY. No.

STRAIGHT A GIRL. I sing. I write my own songs and sing them. Like Fiona Apple.

SUPER ACHIEVER BOY. Give me a break.

STRAIGHT A GIRL. I really love kayaking. Or maybe archery. Or I know, I know: ceramics.

SUPER ACHIEVER BOY. What is this? Things I did at summer camp?

STRAIGHT A GIRL. Fine. If you're so smart, what's your special skill?

SUPER ACHIEVER BOY. I don't know. It's gotta be something original, something nobody else has ever done before, something totally unique.

STRAIGHT A GIRL. Like what?

SUPER ACHIEVER BOY. I don't know. Like maybe if you invented something.

STRAIGHT A GIRL. Like a cure for cancer?

SUPER ACHIEVER BOY. Well, yeah, that would be pretty amazing, but it doesn't have to be that.

STRAIGHT A GIRL. Well what then?

SUPER ACHIEVER BOY. Like a sentient artificial life form.

STRAIGHT A GIRL. Like R2D2?

SUPER ACHIEVER BOY. No.

STRAIGHT A GIRL. Or like I know, I know: like the androids in *Blade Runner.* Did you ever see that movie?

SUPER ACHIEVER BOY. No.

STRAIGHT A GIRL. Oh my God, I can't believe you haven't seen that movie. You *have* to see that movie. It's like the best movie ever. It's about these androids, and they're like on the run, because Harrison Ford is hunting them down, and they look like totally real, but they're not, they're fake, and the only way you can tell they're not really human, is that they don't have real memories. They're all fake memories that were like implanted in their brains by this guy who made them, this weird, nerdy inventor guy who eventually gets murdered by one of the androids because what he did, when you stop to think about it, was really kinda messed up. I mean who creates like another human being? I mean what kinda nut job invents like another human being?

>   *(Beat.)*

What? You look like you're going to be sick.

SUPER ACHIEVER BOY. What if I did actually invent something?

STRAIGHT A GIRL. Then I'd steal it and kill you and write about it in my college application.

SUPER ACHIEVER BOY. Don't say that.

STRAIGHT A GIRL. Then I would get into Harvard and you would be like dead.

SUPER ACHIEVER BOY. Don't say that.

STRAIGHT A GIRL. I'm kidding. Jeez. Don't be so sensitive.

SUPER ACHIEVER BOY. What if I invented something? What if I invented like this girl?

STRAIGHT A GIRL. Right. How can you invent a girl, if you've never even see one naked which I'm pretty sure you never have. If you invented a girl, she'd be like half girl and half giant inside of your eyelid.

SUPER ACHIEVER BOY. Why are you like mocking me? DON'T MOCK ME!

STRAIGHT A GIRL. Wow, are you mad? I've never seen you mad.

SUPER ACHIEVER BOY. I'm not mad. I'm just a little freaked out.

STRAIGHT A GIRL. Look, I get it. I'm freaked out, too. I mean this whole like college application process is totally freaking me out. And I swear to God, if I don't find a special skill to write about, I'm going to kill myself.

SUPER ACHIEVER BOY. Why do you keep talking about killing? First you're going to kill me, then you're going to kill yourself.

STRAIGHT A GIRL. I don't mean it like for real. It's just like hyperbole. You know, an exaggeration for poetic effect. What's your problem?

SUPER ACHIEVER BOY. I have many problems. I don't even know where to begin.

STRAIGHT A GIRL. OK, look, I know, it sucks. We're not cool, we're not hot, and it's like everybody else is having fun, and we're like celibate and like killing ourselves over these stupid college applications, and we may not even get in, and it's like: Why, God, why? But one day, in the not too distant future, we're going to graduate from this suckass high school, and then we're going to get into a really good college, and then we're going to get like a really good job and become like really rich, and then we'll get our teeth whitened and we'll lose all the baby fat, and we'll buy some really nice clothes, and we'll have famous friends and an artist will fall in love with us, somebody really cool, and we'll be happy. We just have to get into Harvard and everything will fall into place.

SUPER ACHIEVER BOY. How do you know?

STRAIGHT A GIRL. How do I know what?

SUPER ACHIEVER BOY. How do you know life's going to be all perfect and amazing if you get into Harvard?

STRAIGHT A GIRL. I just do. I know. I've never been more sure of anything in my life.

SUPER ACHIEVER BOY. You don't know anything. I'm actually probably going to get into Harvard and it doesn't even matter. Don't you get it? It doesn't matter anymore.

(SUPER ACHIEVER BOY storms off.)

THE SEARCH FOR CINDY

by Tim Kochenderfer

Characters

TIM

CINDY

Scene

Tim has just returned home from the tattoo parlor, where he got the name of his girlfriend, Cindy, tattooed in a giant heart on his back.

> *(TIM admires the tattoo on his back in the mirror. The doorbell rings. TIM quickly puts his shirt on and opens the door. CINDY walks in.)*

TIM. Cindy, I was just about to head over to your house.

CINDY. Tim, we need to talk.

TIM. *(Pause, confused:)* Yes… Yes of course. We shouldn't just sit here, um, silently.

CINDY. No, I mean we need to talk about stuff.

TIM. *(Pause, still confused:)* Yes, I'm sure we'll think of some subjects.

CINDY. No, I mean we need to talk about us.

TIM. Good, because I have a surprise that has to do with us.

CINDY. No, Tim, listen, I'm bracing you, ok? I'm bracing you right now for something.

TIM. *(Oblivious:)* Ok, well it sounds like you've got some really good news, so go ahead.

CINDY. First, I think we should break up and this next part isn't so easy for me. That necklace you got me for Christmas, I had to take it back to get refitted. *(Pause.)* Wait, I think I got those backwards.

TIM. What?! What are you talking about?

CINDY. What, about the break up, the necklace or my sentence structure?

TIM. The break up!

CINDY. Yes, that. I think we should break up. Now, there was something you wanted to tell me.

TIM. Break up?! Why?! Four days ago you were telling me how great things were going.

CINDY. Tim, that was four days ago. I'm a completely different woman now. And come on, we fight all the time.

TIM. What are you talking about?

CINDY. What am I talking about? How about the other night when you said the universe is infinite and I said it ends somewhere after Pluto?

TIM. That was a fight?

CINDY. Yah! I cried when you hung up! I mean, what would we tell our kids when they ask? Mommy says one thing and Daddy says the complete opposite. They wouldn't know what to believe! They'd be stopping at green lights and bathing in dirt.

TIM. So we can't have a disagreement?

CINDY. No! I need you to be exactly the same as me.

TIM. I don't even know what to say to that.

CINDY. That's not the only thing. My independence too. Remember that time you got mad at me because I wanted to go dancing with my friends?

TIM. First of all, we had plans that night, plans you made and asked me to take the day off of work for. Second, you sprained your ankle and the doctor told you if you danced on it you may never walk again!

CINDY. Tim, we should still be in the honeymoon phase, but I haven't been happy in forever.

TIM. What? Just the other day you said, and I quote, "I'm happy and I feel like we're on a honeymoon, perhaps it's some sort of phase." This doesn't make any sense!

CINDY. Doesn't it Tim? Or does it make so much sense that it rocks your world to the ground?

TIM. What? What does that mean?

CINDY. You know how bored I get with stuff. Remember that time I tried to take up tennis? I gave that right up.

TIM. You gave it up because you sprained your ankle.

CINDY. Tim, I think you're an amazing person. I just don't think that we're amazing together. In fact, I think I actually drain some of the amazingness out of you making myself more amazing.

TIM. So that's it? It's over?

CINDY. No, no, no. We can still be really, really, really, really, really , really, really, really good friends.

TIM. Forget it. I've got plenty of friends. The last thing I need is one more.

CINDY. Ok. *(She gets up.)* I should go. *(She pulls out a t-shirt from her bag:)* Here, I thought you'd want this back. Go Syracuse right?

> *(She tosses TIM the shirt. He looks at it, confused.)*

TIM. *(Confused:)* This isn't mine.

> *(He hands it back to CINDY.)*

CINDY. *(Pause.)* Oh. Sorry. Can I have a hug goodbye.

TIM. Why? You want one last spin on the Tim-go-round? Forget it sister.

CINDY. Goodbye Tim.

TIM. Goodbye Cindy. Going out with you is like jogging with a lemur. Just when you think you're getting somewhere, bam! You're off a cliff.

> *(CINDY leaves. TIM takes off his shirt and looks at his tattoo in the mirror again.)*

TIM. Crap.

SQUARE ONE

by Mark D. Kaufmann

Characters

DARREN

HECTOR

Scene

The high school's coolest senior, Darren, awakens one morning to find he has been zapped back to being a nerd freshman—the only knowledge the world has of him. Here he angrily contemplates his new "reality" with genuine freshman nerd Hector, who believes Darren has been his best friend since fifth grade.

(DARREN sitting on a bench, seriously depressed. HECTOR enters and approaches DARREN hesitantly.)

HECTOR. You still feeling mopey?

DARREN. *(Not looking up:)* I feel like hell.

(HECTOR decides to sit down next to him. He opens his lunch pail, pulls out a thermos, a sandwich, chips. He opens a napkin and tucks it in his shirt.)

HECTOR. You've looked like you wanted to be left alone the last couple days. *(Beat.)* Since you shoved me.

(DARREN doesn't look at him; HECTOR eats a potato chip.)

HECTOR. I know you didn't mean it. I get real upset about things too. But I don't punch people. I just overfeed my turtle.

(HECTOR takes a bite of sandwich. He keeps one eye on DARREN.)

HECTOR. Aren't you hungry?

(DARREN shakes his head.)

HECTOR. You're going to need energy for the assembly this afternoon. You have to give a speech.

DARREN. Enough with the damn speech! I don't care about the speech. I'm not going to the stupid assembly.

HECTOR. Oh. *(Beat.)* I was looking forward to your speech.

(DARREN looks up at HECTOR; really takes him in for the first time.)

DARREN. Why are you sitting next to me?

HECTOR. *(A mouthful of sandwich; stopping in mid-chew:)* You're my best friend.

DARREN. You have *got* to be kidding.

HECTOR. We've been best friends since 5th grade. It was the day we stuffed those little marshmallows up our noses. We got into trouble. It was neat.

    (DARREN puts his head in his hands.)

DARREN. Oh, God…

HECTOR. Up 'till then, nobody ever wanted to play with me. Or with you. That's what you said. So we were friends. *(Beat.)* And then the other guys became our friends.

DARREN. What other guys?

HECTOR. You know, the guys. Herman, Russell, Petey, Leopold.

DARREN. Leopold Muttmerenzie?

HECTOR. You know *another* Leopold?

DARREN. But he's dweeb central.

HECTOR. To the Juniors and Seniors, I guess.

DARREN. I've never been called a "dweeb" before.

HECTOR. Really? Everybody calls me one.

DARREN. You *are* a dweeb.

HECTOR. That explains it.

DARREN. *(Beat.)* I'm not *really* a dweeb, am I?

HECTOR. No more than any Freshman. I think you're cool.

DARREN. Don't say that; not you. *(Beat, then mostly to himself:)* How did this happen. I lived this already. I've earned my way out of it. I mean, three whole years… I hated algebra then. I hate it so very much more now…

HECTOR. What're you talking about, Darren?

DARREN. *(Beat.)* Hector, if we're…friends…I'll tell you. I gotta tell somebody. It'll sound really crazy, but it's the truth.

HECTOR. You want a marshmallow? They haven't been up my nose.

DARREN. Lose the marshmallows, kid, I'm serious.

HECTOR. Okay.

DARREN. Something really really weird happened to me. I—I'm not really this guy, the guy you think is your best friend. Monday I was a Senior. I was Darren Dormer, but a Senior, get it? And I was…the top guy here. I don't mean just some cool guy, I mean I was *the* guy. And...I must have walked through some—I don't know—tear in space; some time warp. *You're* all the same, but now I'm "Freshman" Darren.

> *(HECTOR has been concentrating hard while chewing his sandwich. DARREN looks at him for a reaction; HECTOR looks back and swallows his bite.)*

HECTOR. Huh. See ya...

> *(HECTOR gets up to go; DARREN grabs his arm.)*

DARREN. Hector, you gotta believe me. Could I make that up?

HECTOR. Yes.

DARREN. Look: my friends won't talk to me. I'm...scared. *(Beat.)* Please.

> *(HECTOR sits back down.)*

HECTOR. Well. You are acting strange.

DARREN. I don't get how you have this memory of a history with me. I only remember my life the way it was.

HECTOR. Well. If this is true, the laws of nature have been broken. Which is really cool!

DARREN. Not for me!

HECTOR. Oh, right. Well...maybe a new reality was created to correct some mistake.

DARREN. It was a mistake that I was a Senior? But why?

HECTOR. Or, maybe...

DARREN. —What?

HECTOR. Maybe this *is* your real life. Maybe it always was and you just dreamed the other one. But it was so real you blocked out the truth.

DARREN. Dreamed it? Dreamed I was eighteen? But why would it seem so real?

HECTOR. Maybe you needed to see what it would be like. But maybe it's better this way. *(Beat.)* Darren, you've just gotta be who you are. That's all you've got.

DARREN. That's easy to say—nobody sees who I really am.

HECTOR. Same with me.

> *(DARREN looks intently at HECTOR as he continues, really taking in what he's saying.)*

HECTOR. Most people see me as a super nerdy jerky dork. But inside I know I'm...Captain Fuselage!

DARREN. Who's that?

HECTOR. *(Mysteriously:)* Wouldn't you like to know? *(Beat.)* And that's how I walk through the day. I live the life of the person I know I really am. *(Beat.)* I'm very happy, you know.

    (DARREN tries to let this sink in.)

DARREN. …There's somethin' in that, kid. Why can't I be the person who's inside?

HECTOR. You're not gonna be Captain Fuselage, are you?

DARREN. No.

HECTOR. Good. Because it's taken.

HEART OF THE CITY

by Eric Lane

Characters

HEATHER

BOBBY

Scene

While excellent at his job in advertising, Bobby would rather be an artist. On a break from work, he visits the massage chairs at a hi-tech store. He meets Heather, a young, enthusiastic, quick-witted, cheeky British saleswoman.

(Afternoon. BOBBY enters the hi-tech store. He looks around, then heads over to two massage chairs, sits in one. He takes off his shoes, which he leaves on the floor in front of him.)

(Bobby's picture I.D. from work is clipped to his bag. He takes out a pair of headphones from his bag. Checks them for 'left' and 'right,' then puts them on for music.)

(He settles down into the massage chair.)

(HEATHER, a saleswoman, enters and goes to him.)

HEATHER. Act interested.

BOBBY. *(Removing headphones:)* What?

HEATHER. Pretend you're interested. My manager's watching… Ask me a question.

BOBBY. Um, does this chair come in any other colors?

HEATHER. The Inner Harmony Massage Chair comes in two soothing colors: sensuous midnight leather and plush dakota suede.

(She gestures for more.)

BOBBY. What about the settings?

HEATHER. The easy-to-adjust massage settings allow maximum—all right. Cheers.

(Her manager gone, HEATHER sits in the chair beside BOBBY.)

BOBBY. That's it…? Aren't you going to try to sell me the chair?

HEATHER. She's gone.

113

BOBBY. Even so. I could be interested in buying one.

    (HEATHER just looks at him.)

BOBBY. I could be.

HEATHER. At $3,000? Not likely. Besides, I've seen you in here before.

BOBBY. So…

HEATHER. Often.

BOBBY. I may've been passing by…

HEATHER. Quite often. Almost every day for the past 3 months, in fact.

BOBBY. Not every day.

HEATHER. No, once in a while you pop over to our store on 57th. You always stay at least one full massage cycle.

BOBBY. Maybe I sat down for a minute.

HEATHER. Usually two. And occasionally if you think no one's watching, three or— *(Notices store manager off-stage. HEATHER quickly stands.)* Comes with four easy to adjust settings:

    (She presses each setting, which BOBBY feels.)

pulse, knead, vibrate and—

    (Manager leaves. BOBBY presses a lower chair setting.)

This morning she caught me writing a poem and has been spotting me like a hawk ever since.

    (She sits.)

BOBBY. What kinda poem?

HEATHER. Just stuff. It's not as though we weren't slow anyway. Sit as long as you want. Your secret's safe with me, Bobby.

    (He looks at her, surprised she knows his name.)

BOBBY. How do you—?

HEATHER. *(She indicates.)* Your employee I.D.

BOBBY. Right.

HEATHER. *(Reads his I.D.)* Stone Advertising—that must be quite pressured. What is it you do?

BOBBY. At work…? I'm an account manager.

HEATHER. Meaning…?

BOBBY. Well, right now, we're introducing a new nighttime shower gel for women.

HEATHER. Sounds simple enough.

BOBBY. You'd think. Only according to my boss, we're not just selling a shower. It's a vertical bath experience.

HEATHER. *(Laughs.)* Yikes! Did you study advertising?

BOBBY. Painting.

HEATHER. What is it you paint?

BOBBY. Not much, lately.

HEATHER. Why's that?

BOBBY. Don't you have to work or something?

HEATHER. I'm assisting a customer. Why don't you paint?

BOBBY. By the time I get home from work…

HEATHER. I think you should paint.

BOBBY. I'm sure there are a lot of things I should be doing but—

HEATHER. A portrait of me. Sitting by a brook, perhaps. Dressed like Ophelia. Flowers in my hair. Light streaming through the trees. Wouldn't that be something?

BOBBY. I'll keep it in mind.

HEATHER. Make you less tense.

BOBBY. Who said I was tense?

> *(HEATHER mimics him with his shoulders tense.)*

BOBBY. Maybe I just have a lot on my mind, o.k.

HEATHER. Yes, vertical bath experiences can be extremely taxing.

BOBBY. Not just… Never mind.

HEATHER. What were you going to say?

BOBBY. Nothing.

HEATHER. Fine. Be that way.

BOBBY. Fine.

HEATHER. Fine.

> *(A beat.)*

BOBBY. Like my mom.

HEATHER. I'm like your mum?

BOBBY. No. On my mind—my mom. Nothing. I'm sure she'll be o.k.

HEATHER. Is she ill?

BOBBY. *(Notices Heather's manager off-stage:)* Your boss.

HEATHER. Is she?

BOBBY. They're just running some tests. I'm sure she's fine.

> *(Notices Heather's manager moving closer. He switches gears. HEATHER rises.)*

BOBBY. I'm definitely interested but $3,000 seems like a lot for a chair.

HEATHER. I don't think of it so much as a chair but as a horizontal massage experience.

> *(BOBBY smiles. HEATHER doesn't turn, but senses her manager leaving, off BOBBY's gaze.)*

HEATHER. Gone?

> *(BOBBY looks, nods. She sits. Simply:)*

HEATHER. I'll say a prayer. What's your mum's name?

BOBBY. You don't have to—

HEATHER. If you'd rather I didn't…

BOBBY. No, I didn't mean… Sue. Her name's Sue.

HEATHER. Sue. Got it.

> *(A beat.)*

BOBBY. Thank you.

HEATHER. Sure.

> *(A slight beat.)*

BOBBY. I gotta go.

> *(He starts to put his shoes back on, gather himself together.)*

HEATHER. *(Rises.)* Off to work. So will we be shipping this to your home or office?

BOBBY. *(Rises.)* I didn't say—

HEATHER. Just joking.

BOBBY. Oh… I knew that.

HEATHER. Of course you did.

BOBBY. Right.

> *(He exits.)*

Read this play at *www.playscripts.com.*

SLIDE/OVER

by Melanie Marnich

Characters

SCOTT, a high school senior.

JAY, a high school senior.

Scene

Scott and Jay are members of a closely-knit group of friends. When the rest of their group departs for class, they sit down to share some coffee during their free period.

Author Note

This play is completely colorblind. If needed, you may change characters' names for the sake of authenticity or to make it right for your school.

Jay is not a cliché, one-dimensional cut-out of a gay girl.

> *(A high school hallway.)*
> *(JAY and SCOTT stay and clean their lockers.)*

JAY. Don't you have somewhere to go?

SCOTT. Not this hour. You?

JAY. Same.

> *(SCOTT takes a thermos out of his locker.)*

SCOTT. Hey.

JAY. What.

SCOTT. Coffee?

JAY. Can you make a double-one-percent-three-shot-soy-protein-with-a-cherry-on-top grande chai?

> *(SCOTT holds up a thermos with a 'this okay?' look on his face. JAY nods, smiles. They sit on the floor a little distance from one another. Pour, pour, sip, sip.)*

SCOTT. How'd your week go?

JAY. Great. Pretty much like any other week. Let's see...
Three new people learned my name...

One guy offered to cure me…
One girl commented on my eyesight…
Only two neighbors talked to my parents without pitying them (that's down from seven at this time last year), one uncle called to say, for the tenth time, that he's praying for me. And I received one letter from "an admirer." Translation: perv. The prank phone call was the best. It took me half the week to convince my parents that "rug muncher" is a new kind of vacuum.
How was your week?

SCOTT. Pretty quiet.

>   *(Beat.)*

Warmer-upper?

JAY. Sure.

>   *(He fills their cups.)*

I saw you and Julia outside today. How are you guys doing?

SCOTT. Fine. She won't be in school for a couple of days though.

JAY. Why not?

SCOTT. She's having about 93 percent of her body waxed. It's like elective surgery. There's a recuperation time. She has a doctor's excuse.

JAY. Women.

SCOTT. Can't live with 'em.

JAY. Can't live without 'em.

SCOTT. Don't take this the wrong way, but…

JAY. Oh God…

SCOTT. I'm not sure we'd be such good friends if you were straight. I mean—

JAY. I know what you mean. Just like I don't think we could be such good friends if you were a girl. Because then there'd be certain…

SCOTT. Factors.

JAY. Options.

SCOTT. Issues.

JAY. Tensions maybe.

>   *(Sip, sip.)*

SCOTT. *(Referring to coffee:)* Good. Isn't it? I mean for it not being a triple-dipple-hum-dinger-double-zinger-puff-ball of a coffee.

JAY. Hits the spot.

>   *(Sip.)*

SCOTT. But then again you're so cool that sometimes I wish you were straight.

(*Beat.*)

Was that stupid? I'm sorry. I'm an idiot. I'll pour hot coffee in my pants if you want me to.

JAY. No. No. It's cool. It's really…honest, you know?

SCOTT. I guess.

JAY. Because I know what you mean.

(*Beat.*)

Because sometimes I wish you were a girl.

SCOTT. There're a lot of things I'd do for you, but becoming a girl is not one of them.

(*They laugh. Sip.*)

(*Holding up thermos:*) Warmer-upper?

(*She holds out her cup. He slides toward her and pours.*)

JAY. Watch *Dawson's Creek* lately? [*Plug in a television show that's current.*]

SCOTT. I never miss it. I like to look at the girls.

JAY. Me too.

SCOTT. More?

(*He pours.*)

That one chick on there's really high maintenance.

JAY. She's my favorite.

SCOTT. More?

(*She slides toward him and he pours.*)

(*Referring to coffee:*) We might as well finish…

(*He slides closer to her and is just about to pour the coffee when they kiss a little kiss. It surprises both of them.*)

JAY. Does that mean I'm straight?

SCOTT. Does that mean I'm a girl?

JAY. I don't know.

SCOTT. I don't care.

(*They kiss again.*)

KISSING SCENE

by Carl Martin

Characters

RICHARD, an acting student.

ASHLEY, also an acting student.

Scene

Richard and Ashley are meeting to rehearse a scene for their Acting Class, which begins in an hour. Ashley arrived on time for the rehearsal and has been waiting impatiently for Richard. Ashley is very prepared and very serious, Richard is neither.

(A theatre. Worklights. ASHLEY is doing warm-up exercises and periodically checking her watch. RICHARD enters.)

RICHARD. Hi. You ready to go?

ASHLEY. Where've you been?

RICHARD. What?

ASHLEY. You're late.

RICHARD. Three-thirty, right?

ASHLEY. We said three o'clock.

RICHARD. Three-thirty.

ASHLEY. Three o'clock.

RICHARD. Three-thirty.

ASHLEY. I wrote it down in my calendar book three o'clock.

(She shows him her calendar book.)

RICHARD. I wrote it down on my shoe three-thirty.

(He shows her his shoe.)

ASHLEY. We said three o'clock.

RICHARD. I'm sure we said three-thirty.

ASHLEY. No.

RICHARD. I guess we have a difference of opinion.

ASHLEY. I guess so.

RICHARD. Should we keep arguing about it or should we start rehearsing?

ASHLEY. Fine. This is the sofa. I start sitting here. That chair is the chair. Coffee table and the door's the door.

RICHARD. We can't have the chair there.

ASHLEY. Where do you want the chair?

RICHARD. If we put the chair there they can't see my face at the beginning of the scene.

ASHLEY. But if you put it over there you have to come halfway across the room when you propose to me.

RICHARD. So what?

ASHLEY. Fine.

RICHARD. It'll be a moment.

ASHLEY. Do you mind if we start now?

RICHARD. You have your lines down?

ASHLEY. Yes, I have my lines down. Do you have your lines down?

RICHARD. Pretty much.

ASHLEY. Pretty much?

RICHARD. Pretty much.

ASHLEY. What does pretty much mean?

RICHARD. Most of them.

ASHLEY. So you're not only fifty minutes late, but you don't even—

RICHARD. Twenty.

ASHLEY. Fifty.

RICHARD. We were supposed to start at three-thirty.

(*ASHLEY picks up her calendar book. RICHARD lifts his foot.*)

ASHLEY. I don't see where you have any room to talk. Even if we did say three-thirty, which we didn't, you're still twenty-three minutes late.

RICHARD. Twenty.

ASHLEY. You show up that late to a professional theatre and it's your job.

RICHARD. This ain't no professional theatre.

ASHLEY. At least you could show some professionalism.

RICHARD. Oh, professionalism. I knew I forgot something.

ASHLEY. Cut it out.

RICHARD. So I'm twenty minutes late. What difference does it make? Besides making you freak.

ASHLEY. We could have rehearsed our scene three times already.

RICHARD. Maybe four if you don't take the time to berate me.

(ASHLEY gives him a look of extreme anger.)

That's good. Remember that. You can use that on stage.

ASHLEY. I don't believe you.

RICHARD. You keep saying we have to rehearse, but you keep stopping to point out my lack of professionalism.

ASHLEY. I'm just asking for a little common courtesy.

RICHARD. I'm just asking you to relax for God's sake. Like it's really a big deal.

ASHLEY. To some of us it is a big deal.

RICHARD. You mean those of us going into THE BUSINESS?

ASHLEY. Those of us who are majors.

RICHARD. Oh, I see. Those of us who are majors are more dedicated.

ASHLEY. Those of us who are majors show up on time.

RICHARD. And waste more time by arguing with those of us who are a few minutes late.

ASHLEY. Could we please just do the scene?

RICHARD. I thought you'd never ask.

(They take starting positions.)

ASHLEY. Scene.

RICHARD. The only answer I can see is for us to get married.

ASHLEY. What?

RICHARD. *(Much louder:)* The only answer I can see is for us—

ASHLEY. We're not starting there.

RICHARD. Where then?

ASHLEY. What did your father say?

RICHARD. What did your father say?

ASHLEY. Wait a second.

RICHARD. Oh, I'm sorry. You have to get into character. Get those substitutions working. My fault.

ASHLEY. Scene.

RICHARD. What did your father say?

ASHLEY. He didn't like it.

RICHARD. The only answer I can see is for us to—

ASHLEY. No. What do you think we should do?

RICHARD. What do you think we should do?

ASHLEY. Wait.

RICHARD. Sorry.

ASHLEY. He didn't like it.

RICHARD. You in character yet? I can't tell if you don't say—

ASHLEY. Scene. He didn't like it.

RICHARD. What do you think we should do?

ASHLEY. I think you should leave.

RICHARD. I'm not leaving without you.

ASHLEY. Go. I don't love you any more. I hate you.

RICHARD. The only answer I—now?

ASHLEY. Yes.

RICHARD. The only answer I can see is for us—

ASHLEY. Take it back, please.

RICHARD. Sorry... Scene?

ASHLEY. Scene.

RICHARD. What did your father say?

ASHLEY. He didn't like it.

RICHARD. What do you think we should do?

ASHLEY. I think you should leave.

RICHARD. I'm not leaving without you.

ASHLEY. Go. I don't love you any more. I hate you.

RICHARD. The only answer I can see is for us to get married.

ASHLEY. Do you mean it?

RICHARD. Gloria, will you please marry me?

(They hug. They look as if they are about to kiss.)

ASHLEY. Hold on.

RICHARD. Script says we kiss twice here.

ASHLEY. I know what the script says.

RICHARD. Let's be professional about this.

ASHLEY. You…jerk.

RICHARD. Maybe we could choose another scene. How long do we have 'til class, an hour?

ASHLEY. Will you stop it?

RICHARD. Now, Ashley, don't get upset. Professionalism, remember?

ASHLEY. Scene.

RICHARD. Scene?

ASHLEY. Scene.

THE LESS THAN HUMAN CLUB

by Timothy Mason

Characters

DAVIS DANIELS, a high school junior.

KIRSTEN SABO, a high school junior.

Scene

It's 1968. There's racial strife around the nation, and a rapidly escalating war in Southeast Asia, but at Nathan Hale High School the urgent questions involve who's in love with whom. 17-year-old Davis is trying to work his way through his own sexual ambiguities by inviting his innocent classmate, Kirsten, to the Sno Daze dance. This date means one thing to Davis and, heart-wrenchingly, quite another to Kirsten.

> *(KIRSTEN sits on a staircase in the school. From down the hall we hear music over the gymnasium PA system, maybe something on the order of a Chuck Berry number, e.g. "Rock & Roll Music" or "School Days" or perhaps the Stones' "Under the Boardwalk," and then something like the Beatles' "She's Leaving Home." DAVIS approaches with hot cider in Dixie cups.)*

KIRSTEN. Oh, thanks!

DAVIS. Look out, they're hot.

KIRSTEN. Steaming. It's my dad's recipe multiplied by a couple hundred. Heavy on the cinnamon.

DAVIS. It smells great.

KIRSTEN. Thank you. I made the fruit salad, too. You're a wonderful dancer.

DAVIS. Thanks, I'm not that...

KIRSTEN. I mean, you never go to dances, where did you learn to dance like that?

DAVIS. I don't know.

KIRSTEN. You're just amazing.

DAVIS. You tired or anything?

> *(Beat.)*

KIRSTEN. My dad helps me with so much, he's such a great guy, I mean, he's a little quiet, he's a mailman.

125

DAVIS. Uh-huh.

KIRSTEN. They tend to be quiet, letter carriers, they think a lot, I don't think people generally realize that.

>   *(Beat.)*

DAVIS. And walk, they walk a lot.

KIRSTEN. Oh, yes. Walk and think, think and walk.

DAVIS. Really. Is there, you know, wax or something floating in your cider?

KIRSTEN. Oh, no, I just knew it! I knew Dixie cups were a mistake!

DAVIS. I mean, it's not a lot or anything.

KIRSTEN. Miss Borders said she didn't think it would be a problem and I said, "Oh yes it will, you just wait."

DAVIS. It's only a little wax.

KIRSTEN. That woman just doesn't listen. Sorry, I shouldn't criticize.

DAVIS. Why not?

KIRSTEN. Well. It's like Thumper's dad was always saying to him, "If you can't say somethin' nice, don't say nothin' at all."

DAVIS. Thumper's dad?

KIRSTEN. In *Bambi*. The movie?

DAVIS. Oh, yeah.

KIRSTEN. It was my favorite movie when I was a kid. Remember it?

DAVIS. Yeah, I think so.

KIRSTEN. If you want to go, Davis, I'll understand.

DAVIS. What?

KIRSTEN. I know you're thinking this was a mistake.

DAVIS. No! Honest. No.

KIRSTEN. You're a kind person, you always have been. But I'll understand.

DAVIS. Hey, I don't know what you're talking about, really. I'm having a great time.

KIRSTEN. You're really so sweet. But you sure as hell don't have a crush on me.

>   *(Beat.)*

DAVIS. I don't think I ever heard you use a four-letter word before.

KIRSTEN. I'm never going to win a Nobel Prize or anything, but I'm not a damn fool.

DAVIS. Wow.

KIRSTEN. Girls. I don't know, they're different. They get crushes.

DAVIS. Boys do too.

(*Beat.*)

KIRSTEN. And I'm not kidding, I think the two of you would be so perfect.

DAVIS. Who?

KIRSTEN. You and Amanda.

DAVIS. Oh, god!

KIRSTEN. Let's go.

DAVIS. No! Kirsten. Please. Let's go back in there and dance some more. Or we could stay here if you like. Talk to me.

(*Pause.*)

KIRSTEN. My dad was so nervous tonight, you'd think he was the one going on a. To a dance. And a little proud, too, I think, you know? But mostly just nervous. He felt better when he met you, I could tell. Did he give you the old third degree while I was upstairs?

DAVIS. No. He didn't say much really.

KIRSTEN. Oh.

DAVIS. I mean, we talked. He gave me a Coke. Mostly he read the paper.

KIRSTEN. I think my dad's a lot more like Thumper's dad than Bambi's dad. Of course Bambi's dad was a great big stag and the King of the Forest and my dad's a lot more like an old rabbit. Bambi's mom died around the same time mine did, I mean, that's about when I saw that movie, right round the time my mom died, and we both missed our moms terribly. I think of all the things I should have said to her but didn't. I guess that's why you mourn. Then you go on. Like Bambi did. This is the first time I ever went out with a boy. I think my dad was afraid I was going to get all twitterpated tonight and that's why he was so nervous.

DAVIS. Twitterpated?

KIRSTEN. You'll have to see the movie. At Luther League at church they pair you off for parties or hayrides but that's different. A boy tried to kiss me once on a hayride but I didn't like him so I didn't let him. There was one boy at church I sort of liked but he moved.

(*Beat.*)

DAVIS. Should I kiss you?

KIRSTEN. I don't know.

(*DAVIS kisses KIRSTEN.*)

KIRSTEN. It's not Amanda? I won't ask. When I talk to myself I sound interesting but when I say things out loud I don't.

DAVIS. I'm interested.

KIRSTEN. And that's a real problem because what you say out loud is important, it's like a bridge, and if you don't have it you're all alone. So whatever you've got to say, Davis, whoever you've got to say it to, you better say it. I would like to go to the girls' room now.

(She starts off and turns back.)

Let me take these, they're undrinkable.

(KIRSTEN takes DAVIS's Dixie cup and her own and leaves. Maybe DAVIS puts his head in his arms.)

AT THE BOTTOM OF LAKE MISSOULA

by Ed Monk

Characters

PAM

JIM

Scene

Pam and Jim have been made lab partners in a biology class at college. Pam has been distracted and aloof because six months earlier her entire family was killed by a tornado. Jim has just found out about the tragedy and visits Pam in her dorm room.

> *(PAM is sitting on bed; her head in her hands, there is a knock at the door made by a drumstick on the stage floor. It repeats the knock on the door at the dorm.)*

PAM. Come in.

> *(Enter JIM carrying the binder she dropped.)*

JIM. Hey.

PAM. *(PAM looks at him for a beat and then turns away.)* Please leave me alone.

JIM. I just wanted to um…I mean…I…

PAM. What?

JIM. I don't know what to say to you. I tried to think of something to say, but nothing…I mean, nothing really bad has ever even happened to me. I can't even begin to imagine what you…I mean you read about things like that or it's on the news but you never….I don't know what to tell you. I just…you just seem so sad and I…want to help.

PAM. You can't.

> *(Pause. JIM sets the binder on the bed and begins to exit but stops. He turns back, looks at her for a second, makes a decision and begins to speak quickly.)*

JIM. We had this dog once, his name was Patches, and he was the dumbest dog in the universe. So one time we had some mice in the house, behind the drywall in the living room, and Patches could hear them. So he would run all along the wall chasing them and then after he got really worked up, he would run full force and smash his head into the wall and then he would stagger all around and fall down.

(There is a pause while PAM stands and stares at him in disbelief.)

PAM. What in the hell are you talking about!? Are you stupid!?

JIM. No, the dog was stupid. There was another time, my little brother had this bottle rocket and he was up on the deck and he was going to shoot it at Patches, who was down in the yard, only he had it backwards, so when he lit it, it shot into the kitchen and went off and scared the piss out of my Mom. So she comes flying out the door and slips on the…

PAM. Why are you telling me this!?

JIM. I don't know. *(Pause.)* These are all my good stories. There's another one about the upstairs toilet overflowing. But that was my older brother and he was drunk at the time…

PAM. So your whole family is stupid?

JIM. Yeah, pretty much. Except for me, I'm the smart one. You can't tell by looking at me, but I get pretty good grades. Well, except for last semester. I got a D in Chemistry. But it was an 8:00 class, so I really didn't actually go that much…

PAM. You got a D?

JIM. Well, technically, yeah.

PAM. I never got a D in my life. My Dad would have killed me.

(There is a pause as they look at each other.)

JIM. Yeah, well my Mom was not pleased at all. *(Seeing and then pointing at the picture on the bed.)* Is that your family?

PAM. *(Pause.)* Yes.

(She picks up the picture.)

JIM. They look nice.

PAM. They were.

(PAM sits on the bed.)

JIM. I've got two brothers like I said, and then an older sister and my Mom and Dad. *(Very carefully, JIM sits on the bed.)* What did your dad do?

PAM. He was a farmer,

JIM. I got an uncle up in Kalispell who's a farmer, he grows…uh… soybeans.

PAM. We grew wheat… My dad…my dad was a *really* good farmer. And my mom, she could grow anything…. She would always have this huge garden and it was just…amazing. She loved to go out there.

JIM. One time my mom spent $80.00 on tomato plants. But by the end of summer, she had only gotten three little tomatoes. So each tomato had cost like 25 bucks.

(PAM looks at him and smiles a little.)

JIM. Told you I was the smart one. *(Short pause.)* Funny thing is, nobody in my house likes tomatoes.

PAM. Do you believe in heaven?

(She stares at him, she really needs to know.)

JIM. Yeah, I do.

PAM. Why?

(JIM thinks for a moment, trying to think of what to say. He stands to say the next lines.)

JIM. I don't know… If you…if you go out by the Flathead River…on a clear night, and…it's so clear that you can see the satellites in the sky…and all of the stars…there's so many of them…it's…it's…so big… I guess… I guess, it should make you feel small…but it doesn't…it makes you feel… I don't know…it makes you believe…that…there's something more…

(JIM sits and there is a pause.)

PAM. *(Looks at picture.)* My mom… *(Laughs)* …just before I went off to college, she got all worried about us needing to spend more time together, so she started family game night. And we all had to play these games together. And my mom loved charades, so we'd play girls against the boys. And my dad and brother were so bad.

JIM. I was thinking about getting a cup of coffee or maybe some hot chocolate. Would you like to go?

PAM. No. *(At first, she is too startled to think about what she is saying.)* No thank you, I'm a little tired.

JIM. OK, sure, I understand.

PAM. But…maybe later. Maybe, we could go later?

JIM. OK, that's good. I'll give you a call?

PAM. OK.

JIM. All right, I'll talk to you later.

(JIM exits.)

COWTOWN

by Allison Moore

Characters

ABBY, 14. Wears cute, trendy clothes. A city kid.

BILLY, 15. Wears Wranglers, ropers, and a cowboy hat. A farm boy.

Scene

Abby has just moved from Minneapolis to an old farm house in Cambridge, Minnesota. The suburbs encroach all around, pitting farm kids against suburban kids at the local high school. Abby wanders into an abandoned barn near their house and is met by Billy, a farm kid who's mercilessly bullied at school.

> *(It is night. Sound of cicadas, wind. ABBY unwraps a piece of gum, puts it in her mouth, chews. She unwraps another piece of gum, does the same. She continues this process as she walks, until she comes to the shell of a barn. She circles the outside of it, tentatively, chewing her huge wad of gum, holding all the wrappers. She steps into the structure. BILLY, until now unseen by ABBY, shines a flashlight on ABBY.)*

BILLY. What are you doing?

ABBY. *(Mouth full of gum:)* Nothing. Who's there?

BILLY. You shouldn't be out here.

ABBY. Billy, right?

BILLY. Place is haunted.

ABBY. So.

BILLY. What's in your mouth?

ABBY. Do you have some paper?

BILLY. Here.

> *(BILLY hands her a piece of paper from his back pocket. ABBY unfolds it, there is a drawing on it.)*

ABBY. But—

BILLY. It's all right. I got about a thousand of them.

> *(ABBY puts her gum wrappers carefully in her pocket, then spits her gum into a corner of BILLY's paper.)*

BILLY. Coulda used one of those wrappers.

ABBY. I'm saving them.

BILLY. For what?

(*ABBY looks at BILLY's drawing.*)

ABBY. It's really good.

BILLY. It's just a sketch.

ABBY. You got the shading for the muscles and everything. It really looks like he's running.

(*ABBY offers the paper back to BILLY, who does not take it.*)

You guys live back over there?

BILLY. Yeah.

ABBY. So what's this?

BILLY. Old Shoewalter barn.

ABBY. How do you know it's haunted.

BILLY. 'Cause, I've seen it.

ABBY. What, like ghosts? Oooooooooooo—

BILLY. You shouldn't be walking around out here. My dad leases this land.

ABBY. I'm not hurting anything.

BILLY. Just because you bought the farmhouse doesn't mean you can go anywhere you want. Mr. Swenson still owns the land, and he leases it to my dad.

ABBY. What, is this like your secret hideout? You do your secret things here?

BILLY. Forget it.

(*BILLY starts to leave.*)

ABBY. I'm sorry. Look, hey. Why's it haunted.

BILLY. Why do you care?

ABBY. I don't. I'm just curious. You're probably making it up anyway.

BILLY. You sure you want to know.

ABBY. Yeah.

BILLY. Mr. Shoewalter shot his head off with his hunting rifle. Right here in the barn. Mr. Swenson knocked the house down a couple years back.

ABBY. Why'd he kill himself.

BILLY. My dad says they were gonna foreclose on the farm. This quarter used to be his. It was a pretty small operation, and there wasn't a co-op then. He left a note for Mrs. Shoewalter, telling her he was in the barn and to call

Mr. Swenson, because he didn't want her to see him with his brains blown out. And he didn't want to mess her carpet or whatever.

ABBY. Did she go out and look?

BILLY. I don't know. She called Mr. Swenson, though, and Mr. Swenson called my dad.

ABBY. When was this?

BILLY. Probably like ten years. I was little.

ABBY. What happened to his wife?

BILLY. She flipped. She opened all the windows and then just left. Didn't take hardly anything with her, my dad said. Went to some home or something in St. Could, near her son. Whole place rotted.

ABBY. I don't think I could not look. I'd want to see.

BILLY. My dad said it was pretty terrible.

ABBY. My dad died, in a car accident. Last August. By the time Trina and I got to the hospital, they were already operating on him. He died in the operating room. So when we saw him, he was already, like, cleaned up, you know? And he looked pretty much normal, cause he didn't have any injuries to his head or anything, his face was just kinda, slack. I think it might make more sense if I had seen the blood.

BILLY. So why'd you all move out here?

ABBY. I guess my mom flipped, too. You got a pencil?

(*BILLY hands her a pencil. ABBY has smoothed the drawing on the ground. She takes one of the gum wrappers and places it over part of his drawing, shiny side down. She begins rubbing the wrapper with the pencil.*)

BILLY. What are you doing?

ABBY. Making a belt-buckle. For the bull rider. See?

BILLY. You got the silver off.

ABBY. Gum wrappers work the best—only the sticks, though. I can sometimes get gold off of like, the Rolo wrappers? But you have to rub pretty hard.

BILLY. Sometimes they tip the horns, too, with silver? Not on the Tour, but other places—Mexico or Spain. The horns suck on this one. I was mostly working on the back legs. I'll show you.

(*BILLY pulls a book out of his backpack, flips through, showing ABBY.*)

ABBY. Where did you get this?

BILLY. Farm auction. It's got cows, bulls, horses—

ABBY. Oh my god, those are naked people.

BILLY. It's for drawing. You gotta know which muscles to draw, otherwise it just looks posed. See how he's using the back legs to take his weight here? And here in this one, it's these other muscles.

ABBY. Yours is just as good as this one.

BILLY. No way. I won't be able to draw them until I ride. Know what it's like up close.

ABBY. Wouldn't you be scared?

BILLY. There's no time to be scared. That's what Cody Custer said. He's a rider? He said you get scared after, when you remember how close the bull was to goring you, or stepping on your chest. But the second you understand how bad it really was, you remember you're out of the ring. You survived. So you always win.

(Sound of a school bell.)

ABBY. Can I keep this?

BILLY. Sure.

TO DATE OR NOT TO DATE

by Jason Pizzarello and Maria Pizzarello

Characters

HAMLET, obsessed with revenge (from *Hamlet, Prince of Denmark*).

JOAN OF ARC, the unlikely war hero (from *King Henry VI, Part I*).

Scene

Hamlet and Joan are on their first date. Hamlet is the young prince of Denmark seeking revenge for his fathers death. Joan of Arc is a young peasant girl who leads the French army to victory. First dates are rough.

Author Note

Every time a quote is used, the act and scene from the character's source play are sited in parentheses.

> *(Lights up on HAMLET, wearing all black, and JOAN of ARC, wearing some form of armor, in the middle of a very polite meal.)*

JOAN OF ARC. Dinner roll?

HAMLET. Thank you.
So, did I tell you about how Claudius, my uncle, killed my father, his brother?

JOAN OF ARC. Earlier.

HAMLET. Did I mention I'm seeking revenge? 'Cause I am, by the way.

JOAN OF ARC. Can't let things like that slide.

> *(An awkward transitional pause.)*

HAMLET. So what do you do?

JOAN OF ARC. I fight in the War of the Roses.

HAMLET. Is that what you *do* do, or do you have a day job?

JOAN OF ARC. No, just that.

HAMLET. That's great. I mean, not many people get to do what they love…
Did I mention I'm currently seeking revenge for the death of my father?

JOAN OF ARC. It was implied. You said your Uncle—

HAMLET. Claudius, right.

JOAN OF ARC. I used to fight with my family, too. That can be rough.

HAMLET. Let me guess. They didn't want you fighting 'cause you're a girl.

JOAN OF ARC. That's sort of frowned upon. I dressed like a boy for a while.

HAMLET. I can see that.

JOAN OF ARC. What do you mean?

HAMLET. No, I…it's just that…

JOAN OF ARC. You think I look like a boy?

HAMLET. No, you just seem…like someone who likes disguises.

JOAN OF ARC. Oh.

HAMLET. You are very pretty for a boy.

JOAN OF ARC. I'm a girl.

HAMLET. No, I know.

JOAN OF ARC. My family also didn't like who I was speaking to.

HAMLET. Boyfriend?

JOAN OF ARC. God.

HAMLET. A lot of people talk to God.

JOAN OF ARC. He was talking back.

HAMLET. Interesting.

JOAN OF ARC. Do you think that's weird?

HAMLET. …No…

JOAN OF ARC. Cool. Most recently, His mother came to me and told me to fight for France.

HAMLET. Really.

JOAN OF ARC. We've been fighting the English.

HAMLET. I think I read something about that.

JOAN of ARC.
I mean, I believe that one drop of blood drawn from thy country's bosom
Should grieve thee more than streams of foreign gore.
                                        (Act III, Scene iii)
But that's just me.

HAMLET. It's nice that you think of a whole country like that.
I'm really focused on my uncle right now.

JOAN OF ARC. What's held you back?

HAMLET. …Well…

JOAN OF ARC. I'm a little surprised you haven't done the deed. I mean, it seems you're pretty determined.

HAMLET.
Seems, madam? Nay, it is. I know not seems. *(Act I, Scene ii)*

JOAN OF ARC. Well, what has stood in your way?

HAMLET. Life is so crazy, ya know? My To-Do list just keeps piling up and then my mother, she's got my two best friends staying with us and once you get started with them, ha, ha…they are characters.

JOAN OF ARC. Hmmmm…

HAMLET. Oh! I did make an attempt at revenge. I did, but he was in the middle of praying.

JOAN OF ARC. Praying? You can't seek revenge on one whilst they pray.

HAMLET. That's what I said!
I'm thinking when he is drunk asleep, or in his rage,
At game, a-swearing, or about some act
That has no relish of salvation in't, Then trip him. *(Act III Scene iii)*

JOAN OF ARC. I see where you are going with this but…

HAMLET. But what?

JOAN OF ARC. Would you mind terribly if I gave you some pointers?

HAMLET. Shoot.

JOAN OF ARC. When you see him next, challenge him on the spot.

HAMLET. On the spot?

JOAN OF ARC. *(As though she's rallying her troops:)* No matter who be near or what his task. You are in the right, no? This is your father's wrongful death, The King, that you seek revenge for?!

HAMLET. Well…yeah.

JOAN OF ARC. Then let nothing hold you back! Show me what you've got!

> *(JOAN of ARC leaps out of her chair with a spoon and assumes an en-garde position.)*

HAMLET. Woah! Right here? Right now? Um… I appreciate your assistance…perhaps we should schedule another time in the future to attempt… how's next Tuesday?

JOAN OF ARC. Are you a man?

HAMLET. …Yeah…

JOAN OF ARC. Then say it!

HAMLET. I am a man?

JOAN OF ARC. Louder!

HAMLET. *(Just barely yelling:)* I am a man!

JOAN OF ARC. This time with feeling!

HAMLET. *(Rising from his seat:)* I AM A MAN!

JOAN OF ARC. Good! Now fight me.

HAMLET. What?!

JOAN OF ARC. Draw thy Fork, you rogue, you peasant slave!

HAMLET. Hey! Only I can call myself that!

> *(HAMLET draws his fork.)*
>
> *(They fight.)*
>
> *(Note: They should fight with the silverware as if they are fighting with Broad swords.)*
>
> *(During the fight, HAMLET and JOAN of ARC get in a tangle that brings them to eye. While they are looking into each others eyes:)*

HAMLET. You are amazing.

JOAN OF ARC. Thank you.

HAMLET. After I get rid of my Uncle slash Stepdad and you complete your war or whatever, what do you say you and I catch a movie?

JOAN OF ARC. I'd like that.

> *(JOAN of ARC heaves HAMLET away. He should knock some things over as he falls.)*

JOAN OF ARC. Viva la France!

> *(JOAN of ARC charges off stage, spoon in hand.)*
>
> *(HAMLET leaps up and stares off after her. He makes a move like he too shall fulfill his mission.)*

HAMLET. On second thought, maybe I'll catch a movie *then* get my revenge.

> *(HAMLET exits slowly with his fork still in his hand.)*

MAGGIE

by Robert Pridham

Characters

MAGGIE

ANDY

Scene

Maggie and Andy have known each other since kindergarten, and always tell each other everything. Now, at age 13, Maggie's become something of a loner, and has been keeping more of her thoughts to herself. Here, Andy takes a decidedly new and unexpected approach to their friendship.

(MAGGIE sits down. After a minute, ANDY sits down right next to her.)

ANDY. Kiss me.

MAGGIE. What?

ANDY. Kiss me.

MAGGIE. Um. No.

ANDY. Um. Why not?

MAGGIE. I'm supposed to have a reason?

ANDY. We're friends.

MAGGIE. That's a reason?

ANDY. Sure.

MAGGIE. Your reason.

ANDY. Sure.

MAGGIE. What about Dilys Braeburn?

ANDY. What about her?

MAGGIE. I thought she was, you know—

ANDY. She hates me.

MAGGIE. How do you know she hates you?

ANDY. Well, she sure doesn't *like* me.

MAGGIE. You gave her a dead mouse.

ANDY. That was four years ago! And it wasn't dead when I gave it to her!

    (A moment passes.)

So do you?

MAGGIE. Do I what?

ANDY. Have a reason?

MAGGIE. I'm working on it.

ANDY. How long?

MAGGIE. How long what?

ANDY. Until you have one.

MAGGIE. What, a reason not to kiss you?

ANDY. Yeah.

MAGGIE. *(Thinks about it:)* Thirty-seven years.

ANDY. Funny.

MAGGIE. You think?

ANDY. You a lez?

MAGGIE. *(Doesn't miss a beat:)* No.

ANDY. So then.

MAGGIE. So then what?

ANDY. So then you can kiss me.

MAGGIE. Let's see if I've got this right. You say: Kiss me. I say: No. You say: Are you a lesbian? I say: No. You say: Then kiss me. Is that pretty much the way this goes?

ANDY. Pretty much.

MAGGIE. Sad.

ANDY. What's so sad about it?

MAGGIE. That you wouldn't kiss a lesbian.

ANDY. Wait—I didn't say I wouldn't kiss a lesbian!

MAGGIE. So would you?

ANDY. What—kiss a lesbian?

MAGGIE. Yes.

ANDY. I never thought about it.

MAGGIE. Well maybe you should.

ANDY. Wait—what if she won't kiss me?

MAGGIE. Then I guess you'd be out of luck.

ANDY. But you're not.

MAGGIE. *(Pause.)* No.

ANDY. *(Suddenly unsure:)* Wait—I mean—you're not, are you?

MAGGIE. What do you think?

ANDY. I asked *you*.

MAGGIE. And I'm asking *you*.

ANDY. *(Exasperated:)* How would I know?

MAGGIE. That's just the point—you wouldn't know.

ANDY. Right.

MAGGIE. So it wouldn't make any difference if you kissed me or not. You still wouldn't know.

ANDY. But that's not—wait, this is getting way too complicated.

MAGGIE. You asked.

ANDY. Yeah. So. About that.

MAGGIE. No.

ANDY. So, then. Okay.

MAGGIE. Okay.

ANDY. I just thought I'd try it.

MAGGIE. Better luck next time.

ANDY. Yeah.

> *(They sit for a minute.)*

ANDY. Jeezer came home from the hospital today.

MAGGIE. Libby Marshall says the emergency squad has a special truck just for him.

ANDY. He's been talking about squeezing up the inside of that old smoke-stack for years, but I never thought he'd really try it.

MAGGIE. So you just stood there and watched him do it.

ANDY. Who was gonna stop him?

MAGGIE. Oh, I don't know. Um. Maybe a friend.

ANDY. Yeah, well, when he gets a plan in his head—

MAGGIE. You call that a plan?

ANDY. Nobody else knew all those bats lived in there.

MAGGIE. Nobody else tried to climb up the inside of an abandoned smoke-stack either.

ANDY. Man, there must have been about a million of those bats. I was laughing so hard the Coke shot out of my nose.

MAGGIE. Nice.

ANDY. Broke his leg in eight places when he let go.

MAGGIE. Well good for him.

ANDY. Jeezer. Effing awesome.

MAGGIE. If you say so.

ANDY. So, wait—you think a lesbian would kiss me?

MAGGIE. You'd have to find one and ask her.

ANDY. How would I do that?

MAGGIE. They say one out of every ten people is gay, so I guess there must be one around here someplace.

ANDY. Where'd you hear that?

MAGGIE. I don't know. It's just one of those things I know.

ANDY. So wait—you mean if I counted up ten of my friends, one of them would have to be a lesbian?

MAGGIE. Probably.

ANDY. You always think you have the answers, don't you?

MAGGIE. There are no right answers.

ANDY. *(Smug:)* Yeah—but that just means there's no wrong ones either.

MAGGIE. Or that *you* can't tell the difference.

(MAGGIE gets up and walks away.)

IT'S A WONDERFUL LIFE

adapted by Doug Rand

from the screenplay by Frances Goodrich,
Albert Hackett, Frank Capra, and Jo Swerling

Characters

GEORGE

MARY

Scene

George and Mary are childhood friends who just got reacquainted at Mary's high school graduation dance. They paired up for the Class of 1928 Charleston contest, only to fall into the pool and get soaked to the skin.

(GEORGE and MARY are walking home after the dance. He's dressed in a ridiculously ill-fitting football uniform, and she's wearing a bathrobe and holding her wet clothes. They sing an old song. GEORGE isn't very good at it.)

GEORGE / MARY.
Buffalo gals, can't you come out tonight
Can't you come out tonight.
Can't you come out tonight.
Buffalo gals can't you come out tonight aaaaaaand
Dance by the light of the moon.

GEORGE. Oh, hot dog! Just like an organ.

MARY. Beautiful.

GEORGE. And I told Harry I thought I'd be bored to death. You should have seen the commotion in that locker room. I had to knock down three people to get this stuff we're wearing here. Here, let me hold that old wet dress of yours.

MARY. Do I look as funny as you do?

GEORGE. I guess I'm not quite the football type. You look wonderful! You know, if it wasn't me talking I'd say you were the prettiest girl in town.

MARY. Well, why don't you say it?

GEORGE. I don't know. Maybe I will say it. How old are you anyway?

MARY. Eighteen.

GEORGE. Eighteen? Why, it was only last year you were seventeen.

MARY. Too young or too old?

GEORGE. Oh, no, no. Just right. Your age fits you. Yes, sir, you look a little older without your clothes on. I mean, without a dress. You look older—I mean, younger. You look, just—

(GEORGE accidentally steps on the belt of the bathrobe. MARY picks up the belt.)

GEORGE. Uh-oh—

MARY. Sir—my train, please!

GEORGE. A pox upon me for a clumsy lout!

(GEORGE picks up the belt and tosses it over MARY's arm.)

GEORGE. Your, uh, caboose, milady.

MARY. You may kiss my hand.

(GEORGE takes her hand, then moves close to her face.)

GEORGE. Hey…hey, Mary…

(MARY turns away and begins singing again.)

MARY. As I was lumbering down the street, down the street, down the street—

GEORGE. Okay, then, I'll throw a rock at the old Granville house.

MARY. Oh no, don't—I love that old house.

GEORGE. No, you see, you make a wish and then try and break some glass. You got to be a pretty good shot nowadays, too—now watch…

MARY. Oh no, George, don't. It's full of romance, that old place. I'd like to live in it.

GEORGE. In that place?

MARY. Uh-huh.

GEORGE. I wouldn't live in it as a ghost. Now watch—right on the second floor there, see?

(Facing the audience, GEORGE hurls an imaginary rock at the second floor of the house. We hear a distant crash of glass.)

MARY. What'd you wish, George?

GEORGE. Well, not just one wish. A whole hatful. Mary, I know what I'm going to do tomorrow and the next day and the next year and the year after that. I'm shaking the dust of this crummy little town off my feet and I'm gonna see the world. Italy, Greece, the Parthenon, the Colosseum—then I'm coming back here and going to college to see what they know—and then I'm gonna build things. I'm gonna build air fields. I'm gonna build skyscrapers a hundred stories high. I'm gonna build bridges a mile long— What, are you gonna throw a rock?

(Now MARY hurls a rock, and again we hear a distant crash.)

GEORGE. Hey, that's pretty good. What'd you wish, Mary?

MARY. *(Singing:)* Buffalo gals, can't you come out tonight…

MARY / GEORGE.
Can't you come out tonight,
Can't you come out tonight.
Buffalo gals can't you come out tonight aaaaaaaaaaaaand
Dance by the light of the moooooooooon.

GEORGE. *(Singing all words on that last note:)*
What'd-you-wish-when-you-threw-that-roooock…?

MARY. Oh, no.

GEORGE. Come on, tell me.

MARY. If I told you it might not come true.

GEORGE. What is it you want, Mary? What do you want? You want the moon? Just say the word and I'll throw a lasso around it and pull it down. Hey, that's a pretty good idea. I'll give you the moon, Mary.

MARY. I'll take it. Then what?

GEORGE. Well, then you could swallow it and it'd all dissolve, see? And the moonbeams would shoot out of your fingers and your toes, and the ends of your hair. Am I talking too much?

CHECK PLEASE

by Jonathan Rand

Characters

GUY

MELANIE

Scene

Guy and Melanie are on a blind date at a restaurant.

GUY. Hi.

MELANIE. Hi.

GUY. It's so great to finally meet you.

MELANIE. Same here!

GUY. So where are you fr—

MELANIE. Wait, before you— Sorry. *(Meekly:)* This is so rude, but the Bears game is on right now? You don't mind if I check the score…

GUY. Oh, not at all. Totally.

MELANIE. *(As she pulls out her cell phone to check her web-browser:)* Thanks. I know this is such an awful thing to do on a first date, but it's late in the fourth quarter in a playoff game.

GUY. No worries.

MELANIE. Thanks. *(As she checks:)* I love the Bears. Great defensive line this year. *(Sees score; reacts a little.)* Okay, I'm done. That wasn't so bad, was it?

GUY. What's the score?

MELANIE. Packers by seven.

GUY. Uh-oh.

MELANIE. Nah, it's no big deal. It's just a game, right? So c'mon—enough about football. Let's hear about "Mister Mystery." Harriet's told me tons about you.

GUY. Man… The pressure's on now.

> *(They laugh together, genuinely. MELANIE's laugh then fades directly into her next line, which is suddenly serious.)*

MELANIE. I'm just gonna check one more time.

(She digs into her purse.)

GUY. *(Smiling:)* No worries.

MELANIE. Is it all right with you if I wear this earpiece? I promise it won't be distracting.

GUY. Sure.

MELANIE. *(As she puts the earpiece in her ear:)* I'm making the worst first impression, aren't I...

GUY. Not at all.

MELANIE. It's just because it's the playoffs. I'm usually normal.

GUY. It's really no—

MELANIE. Come on!!

GUY. What?

MELANIE. Oh, nothing—the line only gives Forte[1] this huge running lane, but he fumbles the handoff. Sure, Pace recovered, but come on—this is the playoffs. You don't just cough up the ball like that. Now you're staring at third and long, and the whole season is riding on one play.

GUY. I hope ev—

MELANIE. WHAT?!

GUY. What?

MELANIE. PASS THE BALL!!

GUY. What's wrong?

MELANIE. It's third and long— Who runs it on third and long? Did Cutler suddenly FORGET that he has an ARM?!

(GUY looks around subtly at the other patrons.)

Oh my God. I'm being loud, aren't I.

GUY. *(Trying hard to be convincing:)* No...

MELANIE. Oh, I am. I'm so sorry. Look, how about this: I'll make it up to you. After dinner I'll buy you dessert at this tiny little bistro on 11th that nobody knows about. I think you'll just—PASS THE BALL!! Jesus, people! It's FOURTH DOWN! Pass the FRIGGING BALL!

GUY. Listen—we could go to a bar with a TV or something.

MELANIE. Oh please, no. I wouldn't do you that to you. The game's pretty much over anyway. *(She takes a deep breath, and is now very calm.)* Okay. I'm done. I got a little carried away there, didn't I? Let's order.

---

[1] Throughout this scene, use position-appropriate names currently on the Bears roster.

(They peruse for a moment, as if nothing has happened.)

GUY. *(Indicating the menu:)* Oh. Harriet said we should definitely try the—

> *(MELANIE suddenly lets out a bloodcurdling shriek and rips the menu in half.)*

GUY. Or we could order something else.

MELANIE. *(Downtrodden:)* They lost…

GUY. Oh. I'm sorry.

MELANIE. *(Starting to tear up:)* They lost. The season's over.

GUY. Well—

> *(MELANIE breaks down, bawling. GUY thinks for a moment, then takes out a handkerchief and offers it to MELANIE. She uses it to blow her nose.)*

GUY. I'm so sorry. Is there anything I can do?

MELANIE. *(Still weepy:)* The Bears suck…

GUY. Aww, no. They don't suck.

MELANIE. They do… They suck.

GUY. They're probably just having a bad season—

> *(MELANIE grabs his collar, pulls him extremely close, and speaks in a horrifying, monstrous, deep voice.)*

MELANIE. THE BEARS SUCK.

GUY. *(Weakly:)* The Bears suck.

(Blackout.)

PROM PERFECTION

by Jane Steiner

Characters

TAYLOR

ANNIE

Scene

It's prom night, and Taylor is picking up his date, Annie. Both have high expectations for the evening, but Taylor is unprepared for when Annie does not react well to the corsage of flowers he has brought for her.

TAYLOR. Wow, Annie, you look so amazing.

ANNIE. Thanks, Taylor. I like your tux.

TAYLOR. Thanks. Oh, I almost forgot. I brought you a corsage.

> *(Pulls a corsage box out of a paper bag, box contains a large, ugly corsage that clashes horribly with ANNIE's dress.)*

ANNIE. Whoa. Wow. Yeah, this is a corsage.

TAYLOR. Do you like it?

ANNIE. Gosh, I don't think "like" is the right word.

TAYLOR. When I saw it in the shop, it made me think of you.

ANNIE. Really. What did you think?

TAYLOR. *(Looking nervous:)* What do you mean?

ANNIE. When you saw the corsage, what *exactly* about it made you think of me?

TAYLOR. *(Clears throat:)* Well, this flower right here reminded me of your eyes.

ANNIE. My eyes are brown.

TAYLOR. I know. And obviously the flower is not, but, uh, the beauty of the petals made me think of the shape of your eyelashes.

ANNIE. Uh-huh. And what about this big, thing, right here?

TAYLOR. Ah, now that is something no other corsage had, so it is itself unique and like no other, like you.

ANNIE. Right. And this interesting ribbon?

TAYLOR. Matches your dress? *(ANNIE shakes her head.)* Compliments your shoes? *(ANNIE raises her eyebrows.)* Bright like your smile? Yeah, your smile.

ANNIE. Did you forget to order the corsage?

TAYLOR. What? No!

ANNIE. Taylor, just tell me the truth. I won't be mad. I promise.

TAYLOR. Okay, okay. I forgot about the corsage until my mom reminded me on my way out the door. I did everything else I was supposed to though. I got the tux, rented the limo, bought the tickets. I'm sorry. By the time I got to the flower shop they didn't have any more. They pulled this one together with extras from a funeral.

ANNIE. These flowers are for dead people?

TAYLOR. No, they're for you.

ANNIE. But you didn't pick them out for me. You settled for leftovers. I'm supposed to be able to press these flowers into a book and someday tell a daughter of my own about all the perfect details of my prom. *(Holds up corsage:)* This won't even fit in any book I own.

TAYLOR. How about a Bible?

ANNIE. My prom memories do not belong in a Bible! Not that I'm saying we're going to break any commandments or anything.

TAYLOR. A dictionary.

ANNIE. I don't want my prom memories to remind me of English class either.

TAYLOR. English class is where we met though.

ANNIE. Fine, maybe the dictionary is better than the Bible, but I don't even know if I want to keep this ugly thing.

TAYLOR. *(Hurt:)* Oh. I understand.

ANNIE. Wait. That wasn't very kind. It is the thought that counts.

TAYLOR. No, it's not. Not when the thought comes at the last minute from your mom.

ANNIE. Okay, Taylor, so far our entire prom date has included discussion about the Bible, your mom, and English class. Maybe we need to just start over.

TAYLOR. Good idea.

(Beat.)

Wow, Annie, you look so amazing.

ANNIE. Thanks, Taylor. I like your tux.

TAYLOR. Thanks. Oh, I almost forgot. I brought you, uh, just as second.

>   *(Takes a single rose from the center of the corsage:)*

This is for you.

ANNIE. Thank you. *(Tucks flower behind ear:)* It's perfect.

TAYLOR. Just like you. Now, why don't we get to dinner. We're probably late for our reservation. What time did you make it for?

ANNIE. Um, about that reservation…

Read this play at *www.playscripts.com.*

WAVE

by Victoria Stewart

Characters

REBECCA, slightly odd, well-meaning, quiet.

CHRIS, her best friend, gothic, geeky but at home with his geekiness, shorter than she is.

Scene

Rebecca, unpopular and practically friendless, has just announced to a crowded, surprised lunchroom that she's holding a kegger at her house Friday night while her parents are out of town.

> *(REBECCA holding a flyer. CHRIS walks up to her, takes the flyer from her. He has a dry sense of humor, likes her. Free period, it's a nice day.)*

CHRIS. *(Looking at the flyer:)* The smiley faces are a nice touch.

REBECCA. It's too much. Isn't it.

CHRIS. No, I'm sure these smiley faces will beckon them.

> *(He holds the paper in front of her face, talking with funny voice:)*

"Hello, come to Rebecca's party!"

REBECCA. *(Amused, embarrassed:)* Shut up.

CHRIS. They're cute.

REBECCA. Thanks.

CHRIS. I don't know why you had to do it at lunch. Announce the party. Why not just invite the people you *know*.

REBECCA. I don't know anybody.

CHRIS. You know *me*.

REBECCA. Other people. People who aren't you.
I'm about to graduate and no one here *knows* me.
I wanted to leave with people knowing me.

CHRIS. You know, if people don't—if they don't show up, that's ok, right?

REBECCA. What do you—

CHRIS. I'm just saying, hey, another night of watching the DVD extras on *Lord of the Ring*s wouldn't kill you.

REBECCA. Jessica's coming.

CHRIS. Oh. Right.

REBECCA. She said she would.

CHRIS. She had that party a month ago and she didn't invite *you*.

REBECCA. That was different. That was a function. For one of her clubs.

CHRIS. Is Amy coming?

REBECCA. I dunno.

CHRIS. 'Cause if it's not cool enough for Amy, it's not going to be cool enough for Jessica. They share the same liver or something.

REBECCA. *(Slightly amused:)* Stop it.

CHRIS. No, really. I think they're Siamese twins, like those Iranian sisters that were connected at the head.

(He leans his head against hers.)

Let's walk around like this for a day.

(She pushes him away.)

REBECCA. They died, you know. Because there was some vein that they both needed. Their mother said that they died happy because it was their dream to be separate.

CHRIS. Maybe it wasn't the dream of both of them. Maybe one of them wanted to be separate and the other would've been perfectly happy to stay as she was. Maybe they had a hard time separating their dreams because they shared the same head.

REBECCA. She's my best friend.

CHRIS. I thought I was your best friend.

REBECCA. She's my first best friend. OK? You know that glass globe on the mantle in the living room? She gave that to me when we were ten. She had one just like it and I used to play with it at her house when we'd play make-believe.
She knew how much I wanted it and she saved up to buy one just like it. So we could be the same.

CHRIS. Her mother probably bought it for you.

REBECCA. She saved up, she told me. So I could have one too. That's the kind of person she is.

CHRIS. That's the kind of person she *was*.

REBECCA. She *said* she was coming.

CHRIS. Then she's coming.

> *(He leans his head against hers, Siamese twin style.)*

Just for the day.

> *(She rolls her eyes and walks offstage.)*

(Walking after her:) Just for the day!

MISS ELECTRICITY

by Kathryn Walat

Characters

VIOLET

FREDDY

Scene

Violet and Freddy are next door neighbors and best friends—even though she calls him her "assistant," in her daily quest to break a world record. Violet's mom just wants her daughter to study her geography and get to school on time.

(VIOLET and FREDDY are on their way to school.)

VIOLET. I don't care what my mom says.

FREDDY. But she's your mom.

VIOLET. Today is special.

FREDDY. How do you know?

VIOLET. Freddy, assistants never ask how, they never ask why—they just make it happen. But in case you really want to know, I'll tell you, when I woke up this morning, I just knew: Today is going to be the day that I break a world record.

FREDDY. This morning I read about the legends of the Greek gods!

VIOLET. I don't want to read about gods, I want to be one, Freddy. A goddess. Or a super hero. Or a rock star—a queen bee. Cleopatra! Or a ninja. Or the world's greatest...

FREDDY. Something!

(They have a break-out dance moment, where VIOLET gets to be fabulous.)

VIOLET. OK, Freddy, what have we got?

(FREDDY opens up the Guinness World Records *book, holding it out to VIOLET, who closes her eyes and points to a page. FREDDY reads where her finger landed.)*

FREDDY. Heaviest Weight Dangled from a Swallowed Sword: "Matthew Henshaw of Australia swallowed a 15.9 inch-long sword, and then attached to its handle a sack of potatoes weighing 44 pounds, and held it for five seconds."

VIOLET. I can beat that!

FREDDY. OK all we need is a 16-inch sword for you to swallow, and then we'll attach a sack of potatoes weighing 45 pounds, and then you'll hold it for at least six seconds—

VIOLET. Maybe we should try another one—just so I can practice my sword swallowing.

(FREDDY opens the book and VIOLET closes her eyes and picks again.)

FREDDY. "Longest Hair: The world's longest documented hair belongs to Xie Qiuping of China, at 18 feet 5.54 inches"

VIOLET. No time to grow my hair!

(FREDDY flips the next page and continues to read.)

FREDDY. Loudest Burp! "The world's loudest burp, measured from a distance of 8 feet 2 inches, read 104.9 decibels—"

VIOLET. That's gross Freddy.

FREDDY. Furthest Eyeball Popper? "Kim Goodman of the United States can pop her eyeballs .47 inches beyond her eye sockets—"

VIOLET. How far is this?

(VIOLET tries to pop her eyeballs. FREDDY measures with a ruler.)

FREDDY. Not far enough, Vi.

VIOLET. Come on, we need a world record that I can beat today.

FREDDY. Longest Backwards Motorcycle Ride? Biggest Cartoon Strip? Largest Slab of Fudge? Greatest Distance Walked with a Milk Bottle Balanced on the Head—

VIOLET. Wait—maybe I can do that. Read on, Assistant!

FREDDY. "The greatest distance walked by a person continuously balancing a milk bottle on the head is 80.96 miles by Ashrita Furman of New York. It took him 23 hours 35 minutes to complete the walk. As Ashrita is a strict vegetarian, he used soy milk rather than dairy milk…"

(VIOLET looks on, and continues to read.)

VIOLET. "Ashrita Furman was born in Brooklyn. As a teen, he was a major geek and bad at sports, but he later came across the spiritual teachings of his guru, and re-named himself Ashrita (he was originally called Keith)."

FREDDY. "Ashrita has broken the most Guinness World Records of any individual! He holds 14 records, including:

VIOLET. Most Hop-Scotch Games in 24 Hours: 434!

FREDDY. Most Rope Jumps in 24 Hours: 130,000!

VIOLET. "Under the instruction of his guru, Ashrita says he can overcome the physical pain and mental anguish of his testing record attempts."

FREDDY. Holy Zeus.

VIOLET. Ashrita is amazing! I don't want to beat him—I want to be just like him.

FREDDY. Be like Ashrita, Vi.

VIOLET. I will, Freddy. OK let's pick, one last time…

(VIOLET does an elaborate physical gesture, closes her eyes and picks. FREDDY reads.)

FREDDY. "Longest Duration Balancing on One Foot."

VIOLET. I can do that!

FREDDY. "The longest recorded duration for balancing on one foot is 76 hr 40 min by Arulanantham Suresh Joachim of Sri Lanka…" You can do that!

(VIOLET balances on one foot, contorting her body and waving her arms as needed.)

VIOLET. I'm breaking a world's record right now—see? Freddy, time me!

FREDDY. I am! I'm always timing you, Vi, just in case.

VIOLET. How long?

FREDDY. Two minutes and 5 seconds, 6, 7, 8, 9…

VIOLET. And how much longer until—

(The ringing of a very loud school bell.)

FREDDY. School?

VIOLET. I hate the fifth grade.

BOY MEETS GIRL: A YOUNG LOVE STORY

by Sam Wolfson

based on a sketch written by Sam Wolfson and Richie Keen

Characters

SAM

KATIE

Scene

Sam and Katie are 5-year-olds who, like everybody, have some emotional baggage. They grow acquainted over lunch and in each other find a reprieve from the dolldrums of everyday pre-school life.

Author Note

The two actors in this scene should not in any way, shape or form try to "act 5 years old," in terms of voice inflection, posture, etc… The actors should just be themselves, and act their age. That is where the comedy lies.

> *(Lights up on a pre-school playground.)*
>
> *(KATIE sits alone and eats lunch on a bench. SAM enters.)*

SAM. *(Saying hello to an offstage friend:)* Stuie! What's up buddy, how's it going? Good to see you out. *(To another offstage friend:)* Jose—como sta, mi amigo? Sweet lookin' Izod, buddy, that's sharp. *(Beat.)* No, they're coming back, they're coming back.

> *(SAM sits down next to KATIE on the bench. He opens his lunchbox and proceeds to eat his lunch. Then, attempting conversation with KATIE…)*

SAM. How's it going?

KATIE. OK.

SAM. Right on. *(Beat.)* How 'bout that coloring inside the lines, huh?

KATIE. Yeah, it's pretty tough.

SAM. I mean, I'm five, I don't need those boundaries.

> *(Beat.)*

KATIE. Counting to 20 is hard.

159

SAM. Tell me about it. Up to 9 it's easy, then you get to the teens and it's just like, woah.

KATIE. And is it really necessary to be tested in front of the entire class. Like I need that added pressure.

SAM. I know! What are we, playing Hot Lava out there?! Save that energy for the playground.

> *(They both laugh. Then have nothing to say. Awkward beat as they go back to eating. SAM goes in again...)*

SAM. And that spelling bee this morning...

KATIE. Oh yeah, sorry I can't spell "parachute" correctly. Like that's really a first round word.

SAM. You totally got screwed on that one. "C-H?" What the hell are those letters doing in that word?

KATIE. I know, right?!

> *(They stare at each other for a beat, then smile.)*

KATIE. I'm Katie.

SAM. I'm Sam.

KATIE / SAM. Nice to meet you.

KATIE. What do you do, Sam?

SAM. I eat paste. That's more of a hobby really. I'm a day trader in the lunchroom. Snoballs, Star Crunches, desserts mostly. And yourself?

KATIE. I'm in sales.

SAM. Oh, what area?

KATIE. Girl scout cookies.

SAM. Really?

KATIE. I'm still just a brownie, but fingers crossed.

SAM. Wow. It is so great to finally meet a girl in this grade who does not want to be a princess. How's that going for you?

KATIE. Please—the cookies sell themselves. In fact, I made a huge sale this morning to Timmy Baker. He bought like six boxes of Thin Mints. He's so sweet—oh, there he is! *(Calling to offstage Timmy:)* Hi Timmy! *(Beat.)* I don't know how they get 'em so minty, they just do! *(Then to SAM:)* He's so yum.

SAM. Yeah, he is. So yum. *(Beat.)* It's too bad.

KATIE. What?

SAM. He got his test results back. Cooties.

KATIE. He tested positive?

SAM. Extremely positive.

KATIE. Timmy Baker has cooties?

SAM. Big ones.

KATIE. He seemed like such a nice boy.

SAM. Timmy Baker? He is kissing girls all the time. His mouth's all over the water fountain. And he's always sniffing those fruit scented markers, that can't be healthy. But I'm clean, Katie. Circle circle dot dot, I got my cootie shot, but Timmy…that guy's dirty.

KATIE. Thanks for the tip. It's nice to meet a boy who's not just trying to get into my cookies.

SAM. Boys can be such jerks, can't they?

KATIE. All I really want is someone to pull my hair, pull my skirt over my head, make me feel special, you know? I'm so sick of these boys who think they're so cool.

SAM. And I'm so sick of these girls where all they care about is, what kind of Big Wheel do you drive, and hanging out in the back of the bus. I've hung out in the back of the bus, it's really not that cool. What am I missing?

KATIE. Most people are so full of doody.

SAM. My last girlfriend was the worst.

KATIE. How long did you guys go out?

SAM. Two hours.

KATIE. That long?

SAM. Yes.

KATIE. What happened?

SAM. Well, in the morning I wrote her a note—I said check yes if you want to be my girlfriend, she did, everything was going great. And then by lunchtime I could tell she was growing a little distant. Then at the end of the day at the carpool circle, she was like, this isn't working out, and I think we should see other people.

KATIE. What changed her mind?

SAM. *(Beat—embarrassed:)* I might have uh…peed in my pants a couple of times.

KATIE. That happens to a lot of guys.

SAM. That's exactly what I told her! Don't get me wrong, I'm in total control now, I mean, I can hold it, but um…she uh…she hurt me really bad. And I just said, no more relationships for awhile.

KATIE. I'm so with you on that. My last boyfriend was just as bad. He bailed right when things started to get serious. One day we were just hanging out, sitting in a tree, K-I-S-S-I-N-G, first came love, then came marriage…but when it came to the baby in the baby carriage, he didn't want any part of it. He was like—hey, I never wanted kids, and I was like, hey, I didn't write the song buddy!

SAM. Well you know what—if he left you for that, then he wasn't Worth it. You deserve better, you're a great girl.

KATIE. *(Touched:)* Thanks. You're a great boy. *(Beat.)* So…what do you want to be when you grow up?

SAM. I'd rather not say, it's stupid.

KATIE. Just tell me.

SAM. *(Beat—embarrassed:)* I want to be a cowboy.

KATIE. Me too!

SAM. No way!

KATIE. Way!

SAM. You're like the coolest girl ever!

KATIE. I know!

SAM. We could be a posse together!

KATIE. I have been looking for a posse!

SAM. This is so cool— *(Looking around:)* Where is everybody going? *(Then realizing:)* Oh…naptime already.

KATIE. *(Gathering her stuff:)* Oh well, I guess we better go lay down.

SAM. *(Hopping up—nervous:)* Woah…

KATIE. No, not together!

SAM. Of course not—you go to your cubby area, I'll go to my cubby area. We're not going to lay down together—that's crazy, right? *(Beat.)* Well, it was really nice to meet you. And I'll see you in PE later.

KATIE. Cool. We're playing with the parachute today. *(Spelling the word:)* P-A-R-A-S-H-O-O-T—parashoot!

SAM. Hey, you're preaching to the choir.

       (Awkward beat as they stare at each other, not wanting to leave.)

SAM. God, I want to nap with you.

KATIE. I want to nap with you too.

SAM. I don't mean that in a dirty way either, I really like you.

KATIE. I like you too—you're just all kinds of pretty.

SAM. But we probably shouldn't…unless you want to.

KATIE. I hardly know you, I can't nap with you.

SAM. It's too soon.

KATIE. If I nap with you, I'm napping with everyone you've ever napped with.

(*Awkward beat as they stare at each other.*)

SAM. I can't believe I'm about to do this.

(*SAM takes out a folded up piece of paper from his pocket and hands it to KATIE.*)

SAM. That's a standard girlfriend contract. Just check yes or no, no maybes! Please, no maybes. Just take your time and look it over—

KATIE. Do you have a crayon?

SAM. Yeah—right here.

(*SAM hands KATIE a crayon.*)

SAM. But there's no pressure to give me an answer now, I mean we just got out of relationships, so if you want to take your time and think about it—

KATIE. (*Checking yes:*) YES!

SAM. (*Grabbing the contract:*) Oh my God—you're my girlfriend!

KATIE. You're my boyfriend!

(*SAM and KATIE grab the rest of their stuff and begin to exit SAM notices that KATIE left some garbage behind.*)

SAM. Uh…girlfriend?

KATIE. (*Stopping and turning around:*) Yes, boyfriend?

SAM. (*Pointing to the garbage:*) You're a quitter if you litter.

KATIE. (*Embarrassed—picking up the garbage:*) I am so sorry.

SAM. It's not my rule.

KATIE. I am NOT a quitter.

SAM. No judgments. We're just doing our part.

(*KATIE exits. SAM is left onstage alone. He holds up the girlfriend contract to the unseen Timmy Baker.*)

SAM. IN YOUR FACE TIMMY BAKER!!!

(*Lights out.*)

A Tiny Miracle with a Fiberoptic Unicorn

by Don Zolidis

Characters

LOUIS, 13, a rather normal-looking 13-year-old boy. That is to say, awkward.

KELLY, 17, Louis' older sister. Big big big unbelievably big hair.

Scene

Louis and Kelly are brother and sister forced to stay in the same room while their grandmothers visit for what proves to be a disastrous Christmas. In this scene they are getting ready for bed late at night. Louis is sleeping on the floor on an inflatable air mattress, Kelly is in her bed.

KELLY. If you look at me, I'll kill you.

LOUIS. I wasn't looking.

KELLY. You better not snore.

LOUIS. God you're mean. I don't snore.

KELLY. You snore. I've heard it.

LOUIS. You snore.

KELLY. I do not.

LOUIS. It's like a motorcycle.

KELLY. You're a moron.

LOUIS. I love you too, Kelly.

(*KELLY throws something at him.*)

Ow! What was that?

KELLY. My clock radio.

LOUIS. That hurt.

KELLY. Really? I'm sorry. Let me make it better.

(*She hits him with a pillow.*)

LOUIS. Ah!

KELLY. Shhhh! Grandma's sleeping!

(She hits him with a pillow again.)

Don't make noise. Louis! Don't make noise!

(She pounds on him with her pillow. LOUIS escapes and fights back.)

Stop it!

(LOUIS manages to knock KELLY over with a vicious hit from his pillow.)

Ow.

LOUIS. Take that, wench!

(She fights back.)

KELLY. Go to sleep or I'm going to knock you unconscious.

LOUIS. Fine. Good night.

KELLY. Good night.

LOUIS. I hope I don't roll onto you in the middle of the night.

KELLY. I'm not talking to you any more.

LOUIS. Good night.

(Pause.)

Hey Kelly?

(No response.)

Hey Kelly are you asleep?

KELLY. Yeah I fell asleep in the ten seconds you shut your stupid mouth. I am not talking to you any more. Do not talk to me.

LOUIS. How old were you when you had your first kiss?

KELLY. I'm not telling you.

LOUIS. Was it with that guy from Wilson?

KELLY. Which guy?

LOUIS. The guy with the little mustache and the rat-tail?

KELLY. No. Gross.

LOUIS. You never kissed him?

KELLY. He wasn't my first. Wait a minute, have you kissed anybody?

LOUIS. Define kissed.

KELLY. So you haven't kissed anybody?

LOUIS. I kissed Rachel Marber on the bus in sixth grade. Well…I mean, she kissed me. And then later I found out that Cass Thompson had bet her a dollar she wouldn't do it.

(KELLY snorts.)

LOUIS. So do you think that counts?

KELLY. No.

LOUIS. Why not? She kissed me.

KELLY. Yeah, but it was on a dare. Like, I bet you won't kiss the monkey over there. Or, I bet you won't eat a ball of cat fur.

LOUIS. Uck.

KELLY. It's not as gross as it sounds.

LOUIS. You ate a ball of cat fur?

KELLY. I got five bucks for it. Shut up. Like you've never done anything weird.

LOUIS. You ate a ball of cat fur and you kiss people and I never ate any cat fur and I never get to kiss anyone.

KELLY. Yeah, life sucks that way.

LOUIS. I'm gonna kiss Carolyn Warren.

KELLY. *(Sarcastic:)* Yeah you are.

LOUIS. I am. I made a pact with myself.

KELLY. *(Even more sarcastic:)* Oh well in that case then.

LOUIS. You don't think I can do it?

KELLY. Like, if you tie her up and knock her unconscious then you could do it. Otherwise no.

LOUIS. Why not?

KELLY. Oh come on. Carolyn Warren?

LOUIS. What about her?

KELLY. Have you seen Carolyn Warren?

LOUIS. Obviously. That's why I want to kiss her.

KELLY. Is she like freakishly weird in ways I don't know about?

LOUIS. I don't think so.

KELLY. Has she called you on the phone or anything?

LOUIS. No. I mean, yeah. One time. For math help.

KELLY. She doesn't like you, Louis. She's cute, right?

LOUIS. Yeah.

KELLY. So why would she like you? She's probably got lots of guys that like her. She doesn't have to settle for you. Not to hurt your feelings or anything.

LOUIS. *(Obviously hurt:)* You didn't.

KELLY. Okay, all right, all right, no need to get sad about it. It's just the way things are. Girls in junior high don't go for the smart guys. Unless they're tall and good at sports. Smart doesn't really get a girl to like you.

LOUIS. What should I do?

KELLY. You're asking me for advice?

LOUIS. Yeah. I mean you've got like tons of experience with guys. Like. Tons.

KELLY. Thanks Louis.

LOUIS. Every week there's like a new guy. It's like you don't have any standards at all.

KELLY. All right shut up. You want my advice? Give up.

> *(Pause.)*

LOUIS. I'm not gonna do that.

KELLY. Well why do you ask me for advice then? You're so rude.

LOUIS. Your advice is lame.

KELLY. Don't ask me then.

LOUIS. I want to know how to make her like me.

KELLY. Either she likes you or she doesn't like you; there's nothing you can do about it.

LOUIS. What if I was like, dangerous or something?

KELLY. It doesn't matter. Go to sleep. God.

LOUIS. Maybe if I—

KELLY. All right, all right. Look: you've got a lot of things stacked up against you—you're a dork, you're ugly, you're stupid, you can't dress yourself, I mean the list goes on and on. But underneath *all* of that, you're a nice guy. So don't try to not be a nice guy because that's the only thing you've got. Okay? And maybe, you know, God will smile on you or something and momentarily paralyze her brain and she'll kiss you. But that's best you can hope for.

LOUIS. I love you, Kelly.

KELLY. Shut up.

LOUIS. I'm going to hug you at the mall tomorrow.

KELLY. I'll knee you in the balls if you try it.

LOUIS. You're so sweet. Seriously, though. Thanks.

KELLY. Don't mention it.

LOUIS. You're the best older sister a guy could ever have.

KELLY. Go to sleep before I gouge your eyes out with a spoon.

LOUIS. Hey Kelly?

>   *(Pause.)*

Kelly?

>   *(Pause.)*

Do you think Mom and Dad are happy anymore?

A Scene for Either

REFLEX ACTION

by Douglas Craven

Characters

ITCHY

KNEE

Scene

Reflex Action is a satire of self-conscious theatre. In this opening scene, two generic characters named Itchy and Knee try to unravel the meaningless mystery of Woodpecker Plateau. They run through some dramatic cliches, use the mime phone which is kept under the blue special, deliver an impassioned monologue and then stichomythize…uh, stichomythiasize…stichomythipate…

(Enter ITCHY and KNEE.)

KNEE. You know, I've noticed that most drama is just two people talking.

ITCHY. Really?

KNEE. Yes, and they generally chatter aimlessly until something happens.

ITCHY. Is that so?

KNEE. Yes.

ITCHY. Except for the occasional long pause.

(Long pause.)

KNEE. Then what happens?

ITCHY. Hmm?

KNEE. After the pause.

(Pause.)

KNEE. I said, "And then what happens?"

ITCHY. Oh, generally a cue.

KNEE. Like what?

(A phone rings.)

ITCHY. I'll get it.

KNEE. No, don't. There's no suspense if you answer it right away.

ITCHY. Oh.

(It rings again.)

KNEE. You know the funny things about phones in theatre, as opposed to the real life phones you and I enjoy and use almost daily, Itchy, is that they so rarely ring at regular intervals.

(He pauses. The phone finally rings.)

KNEE. They seem to wait for the character to finish his lines. *(Long pause.)* And then they ring.

(The phone rings.)

ITCHY. I'll get it, Knee. *(Pause.)* Where do you keep your phone?

KNEE. I keep it over there. Under that Special.

ITCHY. The what?

KNEE. The blue light.

(A blue special shines down.)

ITCHY. I still don't see it.

KNEE. *(Moving to answer the phone:)* Right here.

(He answers the phone and hands the invisible receiver to ITCHY.)

KNEE. It's one of those mime phones.

ITCHY. Oh. I was going to buy one of those m'self. Hello? Yes? Yes? Really? When? Well!

(He hangs up.)

KNEE. You know, it's strange that you didn't give him time to answer any of your questions.

ITCHY. Yes, wasn't it? Even more strangely, I heard everything he said.

KNEE. Who was it?

ITCHY. It was my Arch-Nemesis, Professor Unfrenabulous, Master of the Dark Domain.

KNEE. How did he get my number?

ITCHY. I have "Call Forwarding."

KNEE. Ah.

ITCHY. Well, you don't want to miss an important call like that one.

KNEE. What did he say?

ITCHY. He just called to introduce The Conflict. He's planning to drop by later with his Hideous Army of the Putrefying Undead. He says that he will have some information that will be of great interest to me, and that he plans to wreak horrible revenge on me and to torment and kill us both. And then the zombies will eat our eyeballs.

KNEE. Well! What an interesting and dare I say Dramatic Premise!

ITCHY. I know. If this were a play, which it is not, but is, in fact, real life, we could now do a number of things.

KNEE. What are our options?

ITCHY. Well, we could become more and more tense as the pressure wears at us, until finally the thin veneer of Western civilization peels away, leaving us shouting at each other in a feral sort of way.

KNEE. Never happen.

ITCHY. Yes, it could.

KNEE. No.

ITCHY. I said, "Yes."

KNEE. How would you know?

ITCHY. I do have a Masters degree, you know. I majored in Pinter.

KNEE. Always dragging out that damned degree, aren't you, Itchy? You know, I'm sick of hearing about it.

ITCHY. I'm sick of your resentment!

KNEE. I advance on you!

ITCHY. I respond!

KNEE. I'm sick of your superior attitude. Why don't you just cut out this crap—this CRAP!—and reveal the hidden underpinnings of our relationship?

ITCHY. All right! I will! Ever since I got drunk at that Frat Party and my boyhood sweetheart lost her virginity to another man on the same day that my father gambled away the family homestead while drunk on overproof rum, and YOU failed to assuage my wounded soul and live up to my lofty hero worship of you, I have felt…less than adequate.

KNEE. I had no idea. Is it too painful to discuss?

ITCHY. Very nearly. It makes me want to pause.

    (Pause.)

KNEE. The man who—with your sweetheart…who won your family farm, was he…could he have been…Professor Unf—

ITCHY. Don't! Don't go on!

KNEE. I'm sorry. I'll comfort you during a long pause.

    (He comforts him during a long pause.)

ITCHY. Thank you. That was cathartic.

KNEE. For me, too. How about we introduce a new element? What else would we do if we were in a theatre, which, of course, we are not in. And if there were an audience watching us, which, obviously, there is not one.

ITCHY / KNEE. Let's think.

> *(They think.)*

ITCHY. We could resort to speaking to each other in short lines.

KNEE. Ah. Stichomythia.

ITCHY. I beg your pardon?

KNEE. Stichomythia?

ITCHY. What?

KNEE. Sticho—

ITCHY. —mythia?

KNEE. No.

ITCHY. Yes.

KNEE. No.

ITCHY. Yes. Why?

KNEE. Why?

ITCHY. Yes.

KNEE. 'Cuz.

ITCHY. Ah.

KNEE. Understand?

ITCHY. I don't—

KNEE. —don't see.

ITCHY. Never say

KNEE. That? Never?

ITCHY. Say? Never see!

KNEE. See never?

ITCHY. *(Making wavy motions with his hands:)* Never sea.

KNEE. Yes.

ITCHY. No, no.

ITCHY / KNEE. Long pause.

> *(Long pause.)*

KNEE. Woodpecker.

ITCHY. Wood pecker?

KNEE. No. No woodpecker.

ITCHY. What?

KNEE. Never, see?

ITCHY. Never. See.

KNEE. Woodpecker. Never.

ITCHY. Uh… *(Pause.)* Sorry. Are we still…stichomythicizing? I was enjoying it until the woodpecker. What woodpecker?

KNEE. It all happened so long ago. Do you mind if I deliver a monologue about it?

ITCHY. Go ahead. You were really patient with my Pinter thing.

KNEE. Thanks. Long ago, I was small. It's funny, isn't it, how we start out small and then we grow bigger? So many important things happen when you are small. So many things happen for the first time not long after you are born. Well, I lived in Northern Ontario, where I could hear the sounds of the loons *(Waits for the sound effect:)* and the wind amongst the pines. *(Again. He moves DC. The light favours him.)* I used to live in an old-fashioned place, where you would often hear the sound of an old fiddle player adding atmosphere. *(Fiddle music.)* The place was called Woodpecker Plateau. Do you know, I used to wonder why they called it that. So, I asked my brother. "Why?" I asked him. "Why is this place called Woodpecker Plateau?" He did not know. I asked my father and my mother. When I was small, they were very big. I felt sure that they would know. "Why is this town, this small town in Ontario, with the rustic ambiance, called Woodpecker Plateau?" Their answer seems to echo in my mind, even as I say it. *(Man and woman's voices echo his lines as he speaks:)* "We do not know, Knee," they said. "It's just called that. It's just called that!" To this day, it plagues me. It jumps on my brain when I least expect, causing me to emote, to *emote*! Woodpecker Plateau! Woodpecker Plateau! Even as I enunciate its consonants clearly, it torments me. Wuuh. Ppppppuh. Wwwooddd Pppeckkkerrr. When I eat. When I sleep. When I make love to a woman. Woodpecker Plateau! Woodpecker—! But there was not a plateau, Itchy. And there was not! a single! woodpecker!! Ever! Not a single one. Do you see now? Do you see?

(He appeals to ITCHY, who has fallen asleep.)

Read this play at *www.playscripts.com.*

Also from *Actor's Choice:*

Actor's Choice: Monologues for Teens
Actor's Choice: Monologues for Women
Actor's Choice: Monologues for Men

Edited by Erin Detrick
Foreword by Broadway casting director Kate Schwabe

Discover a monologue book like no other. The Actor's Choice series was carefully designed to help the savvy actor shine at auditions and get the part. Not only does each book give you an extraordinary array of cutting-edge new monologues, but unlike other monologue books, the source of every monologue is easily accessible—each play is available through one website, where you can read nearly the entire published script online for free. Explore the work of today's most celebrated theatrical voices, including Pulitzer Prize winner David Lindsay-Abaire, Naomi Iizuka, Jane Martin, Jeffrey Hatcher, Lynn Nottage, Tony Award® winner David Henry Hwang, and many more!

"Actor's Choice: Monologues for Teens *is an excellent monologue book for middle and high school students with applications for competition as well as use in drama, speech, or English classes.*"

—*The Midwest Book Review*

Order online at: **www.playscripts.com**